THE CENTERS OF CIVILIZATION SERIES

MOSCOW

AND THE ROOTS OF RUSSIAN CULTURE

Moscow

AND THE ROOTS
OF RUSSIAN CULTURE

BY ARTHUR VOYCE

University of Oklahoma Press   :   Norman

BY ARTHUR VOYCE

Russian Architecture:
Trends in Nationalism and Modernism (New York, 1948)

The Moscow Kremlin;
Its History, Architecture, and Art Treasures (Berkeley, 1954)

Moscow and the Roots of Russian Culture (Norman, 1964)

Library of Congress Catalog Card Number: 64-13592

TO CHARLES AND RUTH

I N writing this book I have hoped to fill, in some measure, the existing need for a discussion of the cultural and artistic traditions which dominated Russia in the age of early nationalism. The period under consideration is nearly four centuries long and in a broad sense covers the age during which the national culture embodied a certain unity and homogeneity, when the foundations of the national life were identical for all classes of Russian society. Centered in Old Moscow, the traditions, the evolutionary and revolutionary impulses of the age, its experiments and achievements in all spheres of culture were destined to influence the art and architecture of the post-Petrine and Soviet periods.

Classicism and neoclassicism, which dominated the Russian artistic field during the second half of the eighteenth century and the first three decades of the nineteenth, began to seem foreign, imported. Instead the Russian architects and painters of the 1830's began to look to the national forms in architecture and iconography. Official nationalism and the growing tide of Slavophilism—two currents running parallel but issuing from different political and social sources —were instrumental in arresting the tide of Western classicism and turning the aspirations of the Russian intelligentsia toward the interrupted development of national art. Old Moscow with its monuments embodying the forms and expressing the spirit of national art became the source of artistic inspiration. It was the turning away from St. Petersburg, the citadel of Western culture, to Mother Moscow, the stronghold of nationalism, and the rediscovery of Russian medieval architecture, frescoes, and icons that prepared the way for a nationally inspired modern school of Russian art.

In conformity with the idea behind the Centers of Civilization Series as conceived by the University of Oklahoma Press, I have tried to provide a brief account of certain distinctive features of Muscovite society as it existed in the age of early nationalism and to single out the principal elements and a few of the leading figures that contributed to the greatness of the city and to its role in shaping the cultural and artistic traditions of pre-Petrine Russia.

The space accorded in these pages to the aesthetic element may appear excessive, but in Old Russian culture this element notably predominated. The real expression of the creative genius of Muscovite Russia is its architecture, painting, and the decorative arts. As the present book afforded an opportunity to shed some light on the much debated question of Old Russia's "intellectual silence," it seemed appropriate to dwell at some length on these subjects.

It should be mentioned in passing that since this book constitutes a sequel to my book *The Moscow Kremlin,* there are a few unavoidable repetitions involved in some of the chapters of the earlier and present volumes. In a few instances I have borrowed from my own previous writings, particularly from my book on the Kremlin and articles on Russian art and architecture, without identifying such passages and quotations.

Preface

For the general historical setting I have gone to the classic Russian secondary sources, above all to N. M. Karamzin, V. O. Kliuchevsky, and to volumes II, III, and IV by Professor G. Vernadsky in the Yale *History of Russia.* For the features of Muscovite society I have drawn upon the most diverse material, among which I would like to mention the writings of R. Chancellor, Baron S. von Herberstein, A. Olearius, Paul of Aleppo, P. Miliukov, and D. S. Mirsky. For the history of the city and its daily life my account is based on the studies (in Russian) of M. Bogoslovsky, S. K. Bogoyavlensky, V. V. Nechaev, M. N. Tikhomirov, and I. Zabelin. For art and architecture I should like to single out the works (in Russian) of I. E. Grabar, V. N. Lazarev, P. N. Maksimov, G. A. Novitsky, M. M. Postnikova-Loseva, and N. N. Voronin. To all of those whose works I have used I gratefully acknowledge my indebtedness.

The remarks of S. von Herberstein concerning the observation of Lent by the Russians (p. 63) are reproduced from the translation of his work, *Commentaries on Muscovite Affairs,* by kind permission of the translator and editor, Professor Oswald P. Backus III. Alfred A. Knopf, Publisher, generously granted permission for reprint of the description of Muscovite street brawls by S. von Herberstein (p. 90–91) as cited by Hans von Eckardt in his book *Ivan the Terrible,* translated by Catherine Alison Philips.

My sincere thanks for assistance are extended to the following persons: Professor A. P. Smirnov, scientific director of the State Historical Museum, Moscow, for providing me with illustrations and a number of works by the Museum staff on the history of Moscow; Professor M. N. Tikhomirov of the Moscow University, who has generously given me of his time, suggestions, and his published materials on the subject;

Mrs. Arline B. Paul, head of the reference division, Hoover Library, and Mr. Joseph A. Belloli, chief librarian of the humanities and social science division of the Stanford University Library, for the help and facilities with which they provided me in the course of my studies and for placing so much valuable material at my disposal. I am especially grateful to my friend Mr. Adolph E. Anderson for reading the manuscript, for his constructive criticism, and for valuable suggestions.

Arthur Voyce

SAN FRANCISCO, CALIFORNIA
APRIL 6, 1964

CONTENTS

MOSCOW

AND THE ROOTS OF RUSSIAN CULTURE

CHAPTER ONE

MOSCOW IN HISTORY

From Rural Village to National Capital (1147–1462)

AT the beginning of the twelfth century the political and cultural center of pre-Mongolian Russia began to shift toward the northeast. Under pressure by the nomads of the Steppes, the Russians began to migrate from the lands of the Dnieper Basin to the forest regions of the upper Volga, most of them settling in the triangle formed by the upper Volga and the Oka, comprising the pre-revolutionary provinces of Moscow, Vladimir, Kostroma, Yaroslav, and Tver and the district of the White Lake. Although colonization of the Volga began in the first decades of the eleventh century, the greatest activity dates from the middle of the twelfth century, when the various settlements coalesced into the principality of Vladimir-Suzdal, opening the Moscow era.

The newcomers completely changed the complexion of this area, previously occupied by Finnish tribes. It became the Slavic-Finnish melting pot, and the mixture of the Slavic settlers with the Finns eventually brought into existence the "Great Russian" (*Velikorussian*) branch of the eastern Slavs who assumed state leadership in the Muscovite period. Many national characteristics of the "Great Russians" can be explained by the Finnish strain in their blood.

This migration was one of the most important forces in

3

the history of Russian civilization. Kiev and Novgorod had been, up to the very end of the twelfth century, under the influence of Byzantium. This influence markedly declined in the Volga region.

"Mother Volga" (*Matushka Volga*, as this central artery of the country is affectionately known in folklore and folk-song) played a prominent role in shaping the destiny of the future empire. The basin of the Volga and its tributaries, the Oka and the Kama, the Russian Mesopotamia, became the nodal point of Moscow colonization, industry, and cultural life. It included nearly the whole of sixteenth-century Russia and greatly influenced the development and fortunes of the land. "From the day that the Grand Princes established their capital on the Moskva, a tributary of the Oka and sub-tributary of the Volga," says Rambaud, "Russia turned to the East, and began its struggle with the Turks and Tatars." Her feeling for a community of civilization with Western Europe, which was so much alive during the Kievan period, ceased.

Kiev's immediate successor as the national capital, however, was not Moscow, which in the twelfth century was still an obscure minor town, but Vladimir on the Klyazma River—the political, intellectual, and artistic center of the Vladimir-Suzdal Principality. The latter was an appanage assigned to Vladimir Monomakh (1093–1125), who in turn allotted it as a domain to his youngest son, Yuri Dolgoruky. During the first half of the twelfth century, many towns were founded and largely populated by emigrants from southern districts of the Kievan Principality. Among them were Moscow itself, as yet an unimportant fortified border village, Dmitrov, Yuriev-Polski, and Tver and Kostroma on the Volga.

4

The name of Moscow (*Moskva*) appears for the first time in the chronicles in 1147, but archaeological evidence indicates that the earliest settlement on the left bank of the Moskva River was established long before that time. Indeed, Arabic coins dating from the ninth century were found on the site of the Church of the Saviour at the mouth of Chertory Stream as well as near Simonov Monastery.

There are a number of poetical tales about the founding of the city. One legend related by sixteenth-century chroniclers tells that Moscow was founded by the sixth son of Japheth, Mosokh, whose wife was named Kva—hence, Mos-Kva. Mosokh and Kva had a son named Ya and a daughter named Vuza—hence the name of the river Yauza that joins the Moskva River a short distance downstream from the Kremlin. Another curious and much revised tale which has some historical basis relates that Grand Prince Yuri Dolgoruky, the founder of Moscow (called Kuchkovo in early chronicles), killed the boyar Kuchko for not showing him proper respect and sent his two handsome sons and his beautiful but evil daughter, Ulita, to the Prince's virtuous son Andrei in Vladimir. Ulita, whom Andrei married, became irked by the unresponsiveness of her ascetic husband and plotted with her brothers to kill him. The murder was avenged by executing Ulita in a horrible manner. Her brothers were also executed and their villages confiscated. The tale, which has all the ingredients of the Biblical story of Potiphar's evil wife trying to seduce the virtuous Joseph, concludes that "God put it in his [Yuri's] heart" to build a city on the site of one of the Kuchko villages situated on the Moscow River bluff, the very spot where the Kremlin now stands, and thus Moscow was founded.

For over a century after its founding, Moscow remained

an obscure and unimportant village of the Suzdal province. It emerged into the light of history in 1272 as a small principality when Daniel, the son of Alexander Nevsky, became prince of Moscow. Daniel increased his appanage by the acquisition of Pereyaslavl-Zalieski from one of his nephews and of Kolomna, which he seized from the Ryazanese princes, and thus became the founder of Muscovite Russia.

Moscow's ascendancy began in the Mongol period, and its dominance was recognized in 1327 when Ivan Danilovich Kalita, prince of Moscow (1328–41), obtained from the Tatars the title of *Veliki Kniaz* (Grand Prince). Later he managed an appointment as general tax collector for the Tatars, thus rapidly increasing his wealth as well as his power. Called the "Consolidator of Russia" by the historian Karamzin, Kalita then extended the territory of the Moscow Principality by purchases and other acquisitions, a policy continued by his successors. Although the city of Vladimir was still the official capital of Russia, Moscow had become the real capital, and Kalita endeavored to obtain legal recognition of the fact.

A decisive move for both church and state occurred at the beginning of the reign of Kalita. From the time of the destruction of Kiev through the continued shock and confusion of the domination of the Tatar Horde, the need had grown to establish a new seat for the metropolitan of the church. The move from Kiev to Vladimir at the beginning of the fourteenth century was significant; the next move, in 1326, from Vladimir to Moscow, was much more so.

The metropolitan of Vladimir, Peter (1305–26), passed most of his life in Moscow. His successors, Feognost (Theognostus) and St. Aleksei, made it their permanent residence. Then the Holy See, and with it the religious supremacy which had first belonged to Kiev and later to Vladimir, moved to Moscow, so that the latter city became the ecclesiastical capital of Russia long before it became the political capital. The church, whose power radiated far and wide over the Russian land from the Holy See, now began to draw the various segments of the country toward Moscow, while the great wealth of the church also gravitated toward the city. Moreover, the transfer of the Metropolitan See gave the economic supremacy of the princes a moral authority that helped to ease the bitterness engendered by their unscrupulous policies. The people began to see in the prince of Moscow not a grasping and greedy tyrant, but a God-appointed leader of the nation.

An important contributory factor to the rise of Moscow was its exceptionally favorable geographical position—at a junction of several highways leading from south Russia to the north, and from the territories of Novgorod to those of Ryazan. Colonists from the southern provinces passed through Moscow and settled in the neighborhood for a time at least before resuming their journey north. In this way the Principality of Moscow was enriched by large numbers of pioneering and enterprising people. The Moskva River connected the upper Volga with the middle Oka, and the Novgorodians used this route to ship to their own territories grain, wax, and honey from the richest sections of Ryazan. Moscow's location also facilitated communication with the trading centers on the lower Volga and the Caspian Sea. Relations with the West were maintained through the Crimean colonies of the Genoese merchants. The city thus became a center of international trade and a source of wealth and power for her princes, whetting their appetites for additional territory.

The cultural development of Moscow had begun long before the fourteenth century. It had its roots in the brilliant culture of the Vladimir-Suzdal Principality of the age of Prince Andrei Bogoliubsky (1157–75), which, in turn, derived from the cultural wealth of Kievan Russia with its many-sided international connections. Important progress was made in the first half of the fourteenth century during the reign of Ivan Kalita and his successors. There were certain features in Kalita's activities that roused the admiration of some of his contemporaries, especially among the clergy. This may be seen in the prince's eulogy, which says that his accomplishments in the land of Rus' were like those of the Emperor Constantine in Byzantium.

The age of Kalita and his successors was a period not only of political consolidation but also of the development of art. The construction of the Kremlin masonry cathedrals and churches was an outstanding achievement in Russian architecture in the first half of the fourteenth century. In 1344 the walls of the Assumption (*Uspensky*) and the Archangel Michael (*Arkhangelsky*) cathedrals were covered with frescoes by Greek and Russian painters. The participation of these artists shows Moscow in a unique double role—as a center of Russian culture and, at the same time, a center of international art.

The cultural gains accomplished in the age of Kalita and his successors were further enhanced in the second half of the fourteenth century during the reign of Dmitri Donskoy (1362–89).

Dmitri was the first Russian prince who had the audacity and the organizing ability to defy and defeat the Tatars. The memorable battle of Kulikovo on the upper Don in 1380, which gained for Dmitri his surname of Donskoy,

8

proved to the Russians that the dreaded enemy was not invincible. But Kulikovo was far from being the end. Dmitri had won an epic victory, but the might of the Tatar Horde was not yet broken. Only two years later, under the command of Tokhtamysh—one of Tamerlane's generals—the Tatars surged forward again across the Steppe. Moscow was sacked and burned, the whole principality was plundered, captives were carried off in great numbers, and Dmitri was obliged to resume the payment of tribute.

It was a frightful experience, but Moscow rose from her ashes and gradually regained strength and importance as the capital city of the Moscow Principality. There was no stopping her economic and political advance. Neither the rival Russian principalities nor the decaying Tatar Horde had the strength to impede her progress.

The city was quickly rebuilt. New large mansions in wood and stone made their appearance. Contemporary chronicles and other documents mention the stone palace of Prince Vladimir Andreevich (a cousin of Dmitri Donskoy) decorated with a mural panorama of Moscow by Theophanes the Greek. The "Golden-roofed" Palace-on-the-Quai of Prince Donskoy, gutted and sacked by Tokhtamysh, was rebuilt and luxuriously refurnished by Vasili I, Donskoy's son. When Dmitri died, the Principality of Moscow was by far the largest of the northeastern states. Vladimir, the former capital, had receded into the background, and the importance of Moscow as the national capital and cultural center was firmly established.

The authority of the Tatar Horde continued for some scores of years. Dmitri's successors were sometimes in open rebellion but more often submitted humbly to the Tatar khans. Submission and a transient acquiescence paid in some ways, for the Mongols undertook to protect Moscow from conquest by her western neighbors. While Russia was working out her unity, the Horde, after the death of Tamerlane in 1405, was torn by internal dissensions and dismembered into three khanates, which were soon to disappear from the political scene.

Dmitri Donskoy is generally known only as a great military leader who organized the resistance to Mamai's Tatar hordes. But there was another side to his activities. Professor M. Tikhomirov rightly considers his reign a period of a significant rise in Russian culture. This rise was made possible by the generation born and reared in the age of Kalita. About the middle of the fourteenth century there cropped up in the Moscow Bogoyavlensky Monastery a circle of learned, aristocratic monks. One of the most notable of them was Aleksei, the son of the Moscow boyar Byakont. Highly gifted and extremely capable, he rose to the rank of bishop and was appointed deputy to the Metropolitan Feognost. On the latter's death, Aleksei, at the suggestion of the grand prince, visited Constantinople, where he was appointed metropolitan of "All Rus'."

Aleksei was undoubtedly one of the best-educated men of his time. The translation of the New Testament from Greek into Slavonic is attributed to him. Greek education was not a rarity in fourteenth-century Moscow, actively engaged in trading with Constantinople and other Black Sea ports. The Greek language was used not only by the clergy, but also by Russian merchants trading with Constantinople and Sudak, a port city on the Sea of Asov.

Moscow's close ties with distant Constantinople provide an explanation of many phases of its cultural life in the fourteenth century. Russian visitors to Constantinople had a chance to meet many other merchants and people of various nationalities. Most important were the Genoese merchants settled in Galata, a suburb of Constantinople. We begin to see evidence of an Italian influence in the Russian icons of the period; and Theophanes the Greek, after painting the frescoes in a number of Galata and Sudak churches, was invited to continue his work in Novgorod and Moscow.

The fifteenth century was a very difficult period for Moscow. The pillage and destruction of the city in 1409 by the Tatar Horde under Edigei, the long internecine wars, the rivalry between the Princes Vasili the Dark and Dmitri Shemyaka, and the frequent, devastating fires and epidemics retarded the growth of the city and hampered the accumulation of cultural riches. But in spite of all that, Moscow was able to extend its power and influence.

Ivan the Great (1462–1505)

In the second half of the fifteenth century, the Moscow Principality was still surrounded by the hostile Lithuanian empire on the west, the lands ruled by the Tatars on the east, and the Swedes and the Teutonic Knights holding the shores of the Baltic. In spite of the century and a half of efforts by the Moscow princes to extend their domains, to unite and consolidate the various principalities into one state, there was still much dissension and strife. Novgorod and Pskov were independent and troublesome. Moscow, with no direct access to the sea, had only intermittent relations with the centers of European civilization.

This was the age of the early Renaissance in Western Europe, the crumbling of feudalism, the emergence of two sharply divided and hostile religious camps, and the beginnings of the national power-states. In the East it was a period of transition from Byzantium to Russia, from Constantinople to Moscow, from the Second to what was regarded as the Third Rome. Though widely separated intellectually, Western and Eastern Europe had very much the same atmosphere; a new age had begun, revealing the first signs of an epoch of reciprocal cultural penetration.

Russia, just emerging from Tatar domination and waking up from a long nightmare, found herself still in the Middle Ages. To achieve unity and progress, a strong and far-sighted leader was needed. The man who was to assume this role and who was to bring his country closer to the culture of the West was the resourceful and crafty prince, Ivan III—whom Karamzin called "The Great Gatherer of the Russian land"—the precursor of Ivan the Terrible and Peter the Great.

Ivan III succeeded in annexing almost all the hitherto independent principalities and cities of northern Russia—Novgorod, Tver, and the minor appanages on the upper Oka. He was victorious in Lithuania and Livonia, and he acquired territories which had not been included within the boundaries of ancient Russia, pushing the frontiers of the Moscow Principality as far as the frozen seas of the north and toward the Ural Mountains on the east. Muscovy became an important factor in the international politics of Western and Eastern Europe, and its importance grew steadily during the reign of Ivan. After the fall of Novgorod, the boundaries of Moscow State reached the Gulf of Finland, and it thus became a Baltic power.

Perhaps of greatest importance to Russian political and

social life, art and architecture, was Ivan's marriage to the Byzantine Princess Zoë, a daughter of Thomas Palaeologue (a brother of the last Byzantine emperor), who had, after the fall of Constantinople, taken refuge in Rome at the court of Pope Sixtus IV. When both Thomas and his wife died around 1462, their children were brought to Rome and left in the care of the Pope, who entrusted Cardinal Bessarion, a prominent Greek scholar converted to Roman Catholicism and an ardent supporter of the Florentine Union, with the task of supervising their education.

On the death of his first wife in 1467, Ivan began to look for a spouse of exalted degree. Marriage to a Byzantine princess, a "branch of the imperial tree which formerly overshadowed all Orthodox Christianity," seemed highly desirable; it would further the aggrandizement of the throne of Moscow and, at the same time, entitle him to the right of administering the Russian church. Although he was fully aware that Zoë's education had been contaminated by Latinity, he swallowed his religious scruples and asked the Pope for her hand. The Pope, who hoped that the Princess would bring Russia over to Rome, eagerly agreed.

The marriage was consecrated in 1472, and Zoë Palaeologue took the name of Sophia Fominichna. With her a multitude of priests, artists, architects, and all sorts of professional people came to Moscow from Rome, Constantinople, and other cities. They brought with them Greek and Latin books, priceless ancient manuscripts, icons and ecclesiastical art objects, thus laying the foundation for the great "lost" library of Ivan IV and the Vestry of the Patriarchs.

Sophia's portrait, brought to Moscow in 1470, seems to have disappeared. On a 1498 Moscow embroidery depicting a Palm Sunday procession Sophia is shown leading the grand princely family. She appears to be pretty, but we do not know whether it is an accurate likeness. The Italian Princess Clarissa Orsini, who called on her in Rome in 1472, found her beautiful, though the Florentine poet Luigi Pulci, who was present at this meeting, described her in a letter to a friend of his as abhorrently fat.

Although the lady may have been less than glamorous, Ivan's marriage to her was a diplomatic triumph. With it the aura of sanctity, which the sovereign princes of Russia had originally acquired from Byzantium, returned in a heightened form. As tsaritsa, Sophia intended to use her marriage to elevate the Tsar of Moscow to the position of inheritor of all the power and prestige which hitherto had belonged to the emperors of Byzantium. She enjoyed the right of receiving ambassadors accredited to Moscow and the opportunity of entertaining Italian visitors and Italian residents in Moscow. The latter called her *"Despina"* (feminine of "Despot"), in the Byzantine fashion, and she appears to have loved that title, as she preferred to think of herself as a Byzantine rather than a Muscovite princess.

Moscow came to regard herself not only as an Orthodox kingdom, but as the exclusive Orthodox state and the depository of the True Faith in the world. This attitude resulted from a number of events and movements outside as well as inside Muscovite Russia, which, coinciding as they did with the consolidation of the state by the rulers of Moscow, made the latter, in Muscovite opinion, the successors of the Byzantine emperors. The first of these events was the Council of Florence in 1439, when the Greeks, in the hope of obtaining papal help against the Turks, agreed to a union with Rome and recognized the primacy of the Pope. The metropolitan of Moscow, the Greek Isidore, gave his assent to the union; but he was deposed by the authorities in Moscow, where no need was felt to seek favors from the Latins. Canonical relations between Constantinople and Moscow were temporarily suspended, for the Russians were unwilling to communicate with anyone who might be infected with Latin heresy. Somewhat later, in 1446, the Russian church was declared autocephalous and independent of the Greek Patriarch—a decisive step toward national independence and toward domination of the Orthodox world.

When Constantinople fell to the Turks in 1453, the Russians preferred to regard the catastrophe as God's punishment for the sins committed by Byzantium in compromising with the Roman Catholic church at the Council of Florence. Byzantium fell, it was said, because it had betrayed the True Faith and embraced Latinity, leaving the Russian church the only independent Orthodox church. Moscow felt stronger than ever, proud of her unshakable fidelity to a faith she held unquestionable. This conviction was strengthened by the rapid growth of the Principality of Moscow, which coincided with the gradual decline of the Byzantine Empire.

Now that all the Eastern states and churches were in the hands of the infidels, Moscow proclaimed herself the successor to Constantinople, the Second Rome. Ivan III, as heir to the Byzantine emperors, became the effective ruler of all Great Russia and threw off the last remnants of Tatar supremacy (1480). This succession of events produced a revolution in the Orthodox world, which was immediately seized upon by the Muscovites and made the basis of their political philosophy. Moscow became the Third Rome, the sole depository of all imperial power and the only receptacle of unsullied Orthodoxy.

The theory of the Third Rome was first formulated by the monk Filofei (Philotheus) of Pskov, who in his epistle to the Grand Prince Vasili III (1505–33) wrote: "The first Rome fell because of the Apollinarian heresy, the second Rome, Constantinople, was captured and pillaged by the infidel Turks, but a new third Rome has sprung up in thy sovereign kingdom. Thou art the sole king of all the Christians in the world. Two Romes have fallen, but the Third Rome, Moscow, will stand, a fourth is not to be."

The new political outlook also derived no little from the late fifteenth-century violent religious conflicts which gave rise to the so-called "Josephite Doctrine" establishing close union between church and state and declaring that "the Tsar was similar to humans only by nature, but by the authority of his rank similar to God; he derived his authority directly from God, and his judgment could not be overruled by that of any prelate." The conflict was at first mainly between the party of bishops and abbots, headed by Joseph, abbot of the Volokolamsk Monastery, who fought for the preservation of all the privileges and landed possessions of the church and advocated the sanctification of autocracy, and the party of the Trans-Volga hermits headed by Nil Sorsky, abbot of the Sorsk Hermitage, who denied the right of the monasteries to own lands and preached asceticism and complete renunciation of the political functions which the Josephite faction was proposing to assume. In the end victory went to the Josephites, who contrived to win the support of secular authority.

Relevant legends were revived, and an imperial genealogy

was later officially devised, according to which the Rurik dynasty was descended from Prussus, a brother of Augustus Caesar, so that the ruling dynasty of Russia was of Roman imperial origin. Ivan III's marriage to Zoë Palaeologue added no little to the transfer of primacy from the Second Rome to the Third. The ruler of Moscow took up the role of successor of the Byzantine emperors and the Roman Caesars, and became the head and protector of the Orthodox faith. The visible signs of grandeur surrounding the grand prince were multiplied. To the orb and scepter and other insignia of the Russian heir to Byzantium, including the cap or crown of Vladimir Monomakh, was added the Byzantine double-headed eagle. Access to the sovereign within the Kremlin walls was invested with an elaborate ritual; the whole cere-monial of the court, thickly overlaid with Byzantine custom, took on a fantastic pomp. For dealing with foreign courts the title of Tsar was assumed; in internal acts this title was accompanied by the word *Samoderzhets* (the counterpart of the Byzantine *Autokratos*). In 1589 the idea of Moscow as center of the one true faith received its final affirmation when her metropolitan was raised to the rank of patriarch with the sanction of the four Eastern patriarchs, who now looked to Moscow and her mighty tsar to protect Eastern Christendom.

The new, greatly enhanced status of the crown had to be made manifest by the embellishment of the capital city. Thus Moscow launched a program of building new and magnificent cathedrals and great palaces and residences com-mensurate with her international importance.

Tsaritsa Sophia enthusiastically supported the vast build-ing program. While she was too young when Constantinople fell to have known the real splendor of the Byzantine court, she was familiar with the magnificent Roman palaces and quite naturally desired to have something similar built in Moscow, both as a means of impressing foreign ambassadors and visitors and as a suitable setting for the elaborate ceremonial at the court.

In 1474, spurred on by his wife, Ivan III sent a mission to Italy headed by one of his boyars, Simeon Tolbuzin, to recruit the best architectural and engineering talent available. Tolbuzin was able to bring back with him Ridolfo Fioravanti of Bologna, who, like Leonardo da Vinci, was at once an architect, an engineer, and an expert in hydraulics, military fortifications, pyrotechnics, and metal casting. Many municipalities and reigning dukes were clamoring and competing for his services, but Fioravanti declined all invitations in favor of Moscow, where, he felt instinctively, there were greater opportunities for a full expression of his many and varied talents.

In 1488, Ivan again sent emissaries to Italy, this time the Greek brothers Demetrios and Manuel Rhalev, to find architects, jewelers, metalsmiths, and arms manufacturers. These brothers deserve credit for securing the services of another great Italian architect, Pietro Antonio Solario (or Solari) of Milan, who was one of the principal builders of the Kremlin. In 1493 another mission sent to the court of Ludovico il Moro of Milan persuaded the Milanese architect Alevisio to work in Moscow.

The Italian architects and engineers were put in charge of the Kremlin reconstruction. The walls and towers of the Kremlin (but not their superstructures) are their work, as is the Granovitaya Palata (the Palace of Facets). The fact that most of these architects were northern Italians hailing mainly from Milan may explain the resemblance of the early sixteenth-century Kremlin walls and towers to those of castles of northern Italy. The construction of the Kremlin cathedrals and churches was a quite different matter. Instead of building them in the Renaissance style, which in Western Europe they masterfully imposed everywhere, these Italians had to follow Russian models and build as their Russian patrons ordered. The Italians in Moscow inspired a reaction against the traditions of Byzantine art and thus served to make Russian art and architecture independent.

The son of Ivan III (by his second wife, Sophia), Vasili III, continued his father's traditions and dispatched a mission to Pope Clement VII asking for co-operation in selecting and hiring architects, technicians, and skilled craftsmen. However, the Pope was in no position to give technical help to Moscow at that time, and the mission returned home with only a few architects and craftsmen.

Like his father, Vasili was an enthusiastic builder. He built many new churches, including the Cathedral of the Archangel Michael in the Moscow Kremlin (the foundations for which were laid in the last months of his father's reign) and a number of new fortifications. A new grand-princely palace was completed in 1508, and Vasili moved there in May of that year. In building and decorating the churches, Vasili, who undoubtedly appreciated art, followed both his religious zeal and his aesthetic urge, always engaging the best artisans available. In 1515 the Moscow Assumption Cathedral was for the first time embellished with murals by a group of artists of the Dionysius School. According to the Sophia Annalist, the frescoes were so wonderfully executed that when the Grand Prince, the bishops, and the boyars entered the temple, they exclaimed, "We see heaven!"

The Moscow Princes and Tsars

Daniel Aleksandrovich (son of Alexander Nevsky)	1272–1303
Yuri Danilovich	1303–1325
Ivan Danilovich Kalita	1328–1341
Semion (the Proud)	1341–1353
Ivan II	1353–1359
Dmitri Donskoy	1362–1389
Vasili I	1389–1425
Vasili II (the Dark)	1425–1462
Ivan III	1462–1505
Vasili III	1505–1533
Ivan IV (the Terrible)	1533–1584
Feodor	1584–1598
Boris Godunov	1598–1605
Dmitri the False	1605–1606
Vasili Ivanovich Shuisky	1606–1610
Interregnum	1610–1613

The House of Romanov

Mikhail Feodorovich	1613–1645
Aleksei Mikhailovich	1645–1676
Feodor Alekseevich	1676–1682
Ivan V Alekseevich (co-Ruler with Peter I)	1682–1696
Sophia (Regent)	1682–1689
Peter I	1682–1725

The Sixteenth Century

To the great monarchies of Charles V and Philip II in Spain and of Henry VIII and Elizabeth in England established in the sixteenth century should be added also that of Ivan the Terrible of Russia (1533–84).

Ivan the Terrible (Ivan Grozny), grandson of Ivan the Great, became grand prince of Moscow at the age of three, and in 1547 was crowned tsar—the first Russian ruler to use this title formally. The official assumption of the title of "Tsar" was an expression of the great historical transformation which had taken place in the political position of the Moscow rulers.

Ivan's true character is shrouded in mystery and the role played by him has been and still is very differently assessed by historians. Most paint him in the blackest colors. Leroy-Beaulieu describes him as a "strange compound of craft, mysticism, inhuman in his piety, monstrous in his atrocities, bloodthirsty in his reforms, bred in the midst of plots and suspicions, possessed of a mind singularly free and inquiring for his time and country, combining the Russian's practical sense with the ravings of a maniac."

On the other hand, the Soviet historian R. Wipper points out that "in foreign historical literature the meaning of the term Grozny has been utterly distorted by its translation as 'Iwan der Schreckliche,' 'Iwan der Grausame,' 'Jean le Terrible,' or 'Ivan the Terrible,' thus emphasizing the accusation that Ivan IV was inhuman. In the sixteenth century, however, the term Grozny (from *Groza*—storm) had a majestic and patriotic ring. This appellation had been previously applied to Ivan III."

Karamzin and other Russian historians have divided his reign into two periods: the first, or "beneficient" period, embracing his minority, and the period of the "reforms," which began after the death of his wife, Anastasia.

Ivan believed himself the descendant of Augustus Caesar and, according to Josephite doctrine, God's vicar upon earth. He assumed the dazzling title of "Tsar" and bitterly fought anything that challenged his one obsessing idea—the divine character of the power and the mission entrusted to him. In his desire to establish an absolutism based on military and financial power and not on the sanction of the scheming boyar cliques and the wealthy monasteries, he reorganized the administration of the realm by dividing the whole country into two sections—the *zemshchina* and the *oprichnina*. The *zemshchina* was to continue to be governed by the constituted authority; the *oprichnina* (from the word *oprich,* apart) was to become Ivan's private domain and his private supreme police organization. For the administration of the *oprichnina* he enrolled Tatars, Germans, and members of various tribes in the Russian south, with many men of obscure origin taking the place of the boyars of ancient lineage. Known as *oprichniki*, these men were dressed in black uniforms and rode on black chargers, carrying a dog's head and a broom at their saddle bow as an emblem of their special function—their readiness to bite the enemies of the tsar and to sweep treason off Russian soil. This regime lasted seven years, from 1565 until 1572.

The whole proceeding was an attempt by the Tsar to eliminate not only the influence of the boyars but also that of the church. In his desire to break the power of the formerly independent princes of the other branches of the house of Rurik, he pursued a policy of grisly terror against the aristocracy by executing hundreds upon hundreds of boyars, their families, and retainers. Some were beheaded, hanged, or strangled—they were fortunate; others, less favored, were burned, boiled in oil, or quartered. Elimination of the recalcitrant feudal princes and boyars and the establishment of the full measure of autocracy increased Moscow's prestige as the only capital of all Russian lands, while the old capitals of the feudal principalities lost their power.

Ivan was one of the first Moscow rulers to appreciate the value of foreign cultures and to discover that the East as well as the West had something valuable to contribute. The conquest of the Khanate of Kazan in 1552 brought into the Moscow State a territory with a relatively dense population of Moslem and pagan non-Russians. By this conquest Russia annexed a segment of the Orient and, with the annexation of Astrakhan in 1556, itself became an oriental state. Muscovy now extended not only to the Urals but to the Caspian. The barrier to the Far East was lifted. The great trade routes that Kazan controlled—the Volga highway to the Caspian and Caucasian markets and the Kama road to the Ural Mountains and the lands beyond—were at last opened.

Shortly after the fall of Kazan, Russia received unexpected visitors from across the seas. The English Trading Expedition, headed by Richard Chancellor, arrived in Moscow to make the first contacts Muscovite Russia had with England. The route opened by the Expedition along the Northern Dvina through Archangel added one more window to the West and provided an opportunity for trade, for greater understanding, and for cultural exchange between England and Russia. The trade arrangement made a great contribution to Russia's economic development, and consequently to its political and cultural development as well. In exchange for a promise to ship military supplies and other goods through the mouth of the Northern Dvina the English obtained exclusive rights to utilize the northern route, the right to trade duty-free all over the Moscow State, right of free entry and departure, and also right of free transit by the Volga route to Persia and Central Asia. They acquired a firm footing, established warehouses in all the large towns, and became the most favored foreign merchants in the Moscow State. In spite of Dutch attempts at competition, the English controlled the Russian market and managed to influence the political thought of Russia as well and to give the nascent process of Europeanization a character in keeping with their national interests. More than this, Russia's attitudes toward the European powers was colored by English advice. Ivan became a strong Anglophile and even considered the possibility of marrying Queen Elizabeth or, if that were impossible, Lady Hastings. He wanted to provide an asylum in England for himself if his dynasty should fall. It is not surprising that he was called the "English Tsar" by his intimates.

The conquest of the Volga trade routes and the coming of the English mark a new era: Russia ceased to be a land of natural economy; commercial capitalism became a dominating economic force. Moscow became a thriving metropolis, the largest city in Russia, a center of trade, religion, learning, and art. The eventful and turbulent age of Ivan the Terrible witnessed not only the great political and commercial expansion of the Russian state, but also the burgeoning of national literature.

About the middle of the sixteenth century, Moscow embarked upon a series of large-scale literary undertakings directed toward summing up the past from the point of view of official Muscovite ideology, first as a means of glorifying the past, and second to demonstrate the continuity of the political and religious process from the beginning of the Russian state and the Russian church down to that day.

The established quasi-official concept of Moscow as the "Third Rome," focal point of Orthodox sanctity, provided the incentive for supplementing the roster of saints—the glory of medieval Russia—and for re-examining the supply of saints canonized in various principalities prior to the merger into a single Muscovite state. After an investigation ordered by the Metropolitan Makari (1543–64), the Church Council of 1547 canonized twenty-two local saints; the second Church Council of 1549 added seventeen. Lives of the new saints had to be written and entered in the *Cheti Minyei* (Lives of the Saints), eulogistic discourses arranged under the dates of the saints' respective feasts.

This work, which contains about 27,000 pages, grew and expanded into a huge twelve-volume illustrated world history executed in the studios of Ivan IV by a large group of scribes, miniaturists, and icon painters, who developed a delicate technique of water color painting. The first three volumes of this encyclopedia contain the text of the *Chronograph* (chronicle compilations); the last is the *Stepennaya Kniga (Book of Degrees of the Imperial Genealogy)*, which glorifies to the utmost the historic past and the present of Muscovite Rus', primarily by extolling the rulers as having acted in full accord with the church. It lists the ecclesiastical and civil events of Russian history from a purely religious point of view, and is arranged by the reigns of the grand princes.

The whole of Russian history is depicted as the history of "Holy Russia" and is identified with the history of the tsars' dynasty—the history "of those in the Russian land who shone with piety, the God-appointed holders of the scepter, who, like the trees of paradise were planted by God." The idea brought forward was a God-ordained Muscovite Empire headed by autocrats who traced their lineage to the Roman Emperor Augustus.

Six volumes of this work dealing with the history of Russia proper contain about ten thousand miniatures depicting the architecture, costumes, utensils, arms, and armor of the age—thus presenting a complete picture of the life, manners, and customs not only of the grand princes and tsars but also of the common people.

The sixteenth century was particularly notable for its experimentation, daring, and novelty. The architecture, the iconography, and the decorative arts were distinctive and highly imaginative. The works of art produced during this period became the nucleus of Russian aesthetics.

An effort was made to evolve a consistent art policy and ideology, especially in iconography. The violent controversy that flared up in church and state clearly reflected the richness of intellectual life and the abundance of talent among the laymen and clerics who surrounded Ivan IV in the early years of his reign. Among the outstanding figures of Russian culture of the period were the printer and publisher Ivan Fedorov; the writers Peresvetov, Yermolai-Erasmus, the Metropolitan Makari (compiler of the *Grand Cheti Minyei*), Archpriest Sylvester, and the Tsar himself, who was a man of learning; the soldier and author Prince Andrei Kurbsky; the metal-casting specialist Andrei Chokhov; and the architects Barma and Posnik Yakovlev, builders of St. Basil's Cathedral.

The first printing press in Moscow began operation in 1563; the first printers were Ivan Fedorov and Peter Mstislavets; and the first printed book published in Moscow,

March 1, 1564, was the *Apostle*. Printing was helpful in bringing uniformity to the chaotic Russian religious literature. Moreover, it became a significant factor in the evolution of a new era by spreading uniform concepts of Russian life and statehood.

The Tsar was endowed with an unusual memory and with no mean literary abilities. He read much and could quote an amazing number of Biblical and historical texts. He was the most literate and articulate of the Muscovite sovereigns. His letters are masterpieces of Old Russian political polemics, bristling with withering sarcasm expressed in pithy terms. One of his best is the letter to the Abbot of St. Cyril's Monastery in which he pours out all the poison of his grim irony on the unascetic life of the boyars, shorn monks, and those exiled by his order. His picture of their luxurious life, gorging themselves with the best of food and drink in the supposed citadel of asceticism, is a masterpiece of ironical contempt.

Ivan read a great deal of Russian history, but he was even more eager to study what was happening in Europe, so that he could vie with the Roman Pope, Western emperors, kings, diplomats, and ambassadors. He sought to come to terms with Europe in his own mind by familiarizing himself with its history and culture.

Many rumors circulated in Western Europe that Ivan owned a large library of rare Greek, Hebrew, and Latin manuscripts. It was said that he augmented his father's library containing the Greek and Latin manuscripts which Zoë Palaeologue brought with her in 1472 by a steady and systematic gathering from all over Russia as well as from Western European and Near East centers of learning. His agents were instructed to procure, at whatever cost, manuscripts of special interest to him. In 1554 he succeeded in obtaining most of the extant collection of Yaroslav the Wise (1019–54), who prior to Ivan IV had been the most cultured prince in Russia.

Ivan was well aware of the great intrinsic value of his library, and in order to insure against possible damage by fire or theft, he had it stored in specially constructed underground vaults. He was also aware of its propaganda value abroad and made efforts to engage foreign scholars to translate the rare Greek and Latin manuscripts in order to show all of Europe what literary riches were stored in Moscow and thus disprove the prevailing idea that Russia was an uncultured and ignorant nation. There is substantial evidence that he commissioned the German scholar, the Dorpat pastor Vesterman (Vetterman), to translate some of the works into Russian, but ensuing events and more pressing state business prevented completion of this project.

This library and its whereabouts have been the subject of speculation by many scholars. Christopher von-Dobelov (1768–1830), professor of the Dorpat University, asserted that he had a document written in German by an eyewitness who stated that the Tsar's collection of manuscripts numbered eight hundred volumes, the larger part consisting of Greek works, but also many in Latin, and he listed the titles. Edward Traemer, lecturer on philology in the Strassburg University in the late nineteenth century, believed that the collection contained among other rare ancient Greek works a copy of the Homeric Hymns.

As one of the first monarchs to make systematic attempts to exploit art for state propaganda, Ivan gave great impulse not only to architecture but to the development of icon painting and the applied arts and crafts. He had a keen appreciation of the arts of the jeweler, the goldsmith, and the enameler, and was fully conscious of their value in enhancing the prestige of his regime. He established a settlement on the outskirts of Moscow for all the German metalworkers who had been captured in his Livonian wars, and in 1567 imported a number of goldsmiths from England. The first mercenaries, enlisted from the prisoners, were the precursors of a long line of military leaders, administrators, physicians, and architects who entered the service of the Russian government (in many instances becoming naturalized citizens) and exercised great influence on the course of Russian civilization.

When he annexed Novgorod in 1570, Ivan resolved to curb its turbulent spirit by transferring its population. Thousands of families were exiled, and many of them were brought to Moscow. These new arrivals included certain Hanseatic merchants, who formed the nucleus of the foreign colony in the capital, which a century later became instrumental in opening a new era in Russian cultural life.

A conscientious dilettante and collector, Ivan had the gift of discovering talented Russian artists and craftsmen, putting them to work, and getting the best from them. He accepted or rejected commissioned works of art according to his personal likes and dislikes. During his outbursts of piety and repentance, many churches and monasteries were the recipients of gifts of icons, iconostases, vestments, and church vessels. The icon encasements, relic containers, ciboria, chalices, and censers made during his reign are among the finest examples of the art of embossing, chiseling, engraving, filigree, enameling, and niello work. Until the closing years of the sixteenth century, when the Stroganovs came to the fore as patrons of the arts, the Tsar, with his immediate advisers among the clergy, remained the chief arbiter and customer of art. By the end of the period the artistic, clerical, and exclusively national spirit of Muscovy had assumed its final form. It remained practically unchanged for another hundred years; even the terrible ordeal of the "Time of Trouble" failed to modify it.

When Ivan died in 1584, Russia was left in a state of moral perplexity and political chaos. His second son, the feeble-minded Feodor (1584–98), was unfit to rule his vast and unsettled country, but his short reign was unexpectedly one of the happiest and the most successful in Russian history. The Tsar himself spent most of his time in prayer and in ringing church bells, but under the able administration of his brother-in-law, Boris Godunov—the power behind the throne—the country enjoyed internal peace and continued its expansion.

With the death of Tsar Feodor, last of the House of Rurik, his successor, Godunov, found himself unable to maintain as tsar the unquestioned authority he had so skillfully wielded during Feodor's reign. He failed to avert the grave social crises which were caused in part by the drastic reforms of Ivan IV. The country became a prey to political disorder and social revolution, aggravated by the invasions of the Poles, Tatars, and Swedes, who used this opportunity for attack upon a once powerful neighbor. Moscow fell into the hands of the Poles, and the rest of the country was laid waste by rebellious peasants or bands of foreign adventurers. This period, *Smutnoe vremya* (not quite correctly translated as the "Time of Trouble") ended with the election in 1613 of Mikhail Romanov, the founder of the new dynasty.

After fifteen years of civil war and foreign intervention— with murders, executions, treacheries, and perjuries innumerable, with the ruin of trade, with the extinction of many ancient families—the city of Moscow welcomed the accession of a tsar who gave promise of order and tranquility. A new Russia emerged with the advent of the Romanov dynasty. The power of the princes and the aristocracy was gone and a new social class had taken its place—a class of service aristocracy consisting mostly of self-made men with a sprinkling of descendants of the former artistocracy, which accepted the principle of service as the sole basis for its rights. This class had decidedly Western leanings and was interested in commercial expansion. The rise of the new social group and the expansion of cultural and trade relations with the West contributed very largely toward bringing about a secularization of culture in the Muscovite state, first in the realm of purely practical affairs, then in the realm of art. Ecclesiastical control of the arts was weakened, giving way to a secular element, now largely imported from the West, chiefly through Poland and the Ukraine.

By the middle of the seventeenth century Russian art turned decisively toward new directions and new ideas. This turn is so marked that it would be quite correct to move back the commonly accepted date for the beginning of the modern period in Russian art (the post-Petrine period) a full half-century, i.e., from the founding of St. Petersburg to the first years of the reign of Tsar Aleksei Mikhailovich (1645–76). The turn began with the appearance of foreign artists and craftsmen in Moscow, who, in larger and larger numbers, found employment at the Oruzheinaya Palata. Here, in this first Russian Academy of Fine and Applied Arts and State Ministry in charge of Military and Civil Engineering combined, the soil was prepared and the seeds of the new aesthetics were sown.

The final phase of the national period in Russian civilization, its aesthetic and worldly aspects, found its truest expression in the person of Tsar Aleksei Mikhailovich, the most attractive of old Russian caftan-clad tsars. He is known in history by the surname *Tishaishei*, which literally translated means "the most quiet" (by extension, "the most gentle" or "the most peaceful"). By one of fate's characteristic ironies the reign of this peace-loving tsar was one of the most turbulent in Muscovite history. Apart from social unrest it was marked by the Great Schism (*Raskol*) which split the Russian church into two irreconcilable camps. It was connected with the movement in the higher ranks of the clergy to draw Russian Orthodoxy into closer unity with the Greek church as a whole, and in particular to revise the liturgies in use, which had been corrupted in the past by copyists' errors, and bring them into conformity with Greek usage. The movement came to a head in 1652 with the consecration as Russian patriarch of Nikon, the most striking figure of the whole Russian hierarchy. A strong-willed man, intensely pious yet arrogant, he changed the whole course of Russian church history, and his place in the life of the country can only be compared to that of another ardent reformer, Peter the Great.

The changes Nikon introduced in 1653 might elsewhere have appeared trivial. The most notable required that communicants making the sign of the cross should join three fingers symbolizing the Trinity, not two fingers symbolizing the dual nature of Christ, which was the ancient custom in Russia. But change in any form flouted the theory of Moscow as the Third Rome—the old conviction that Russian Orthodoxy alone was the True Faith, and that not a single iota of its dogma and ritual might be changed.

As a result, there was a violent reaction to the change in

ritual. It became a burning issue within the church and was more important to the people than the reform of the service books carried through by Nikon. In 1654 a Church Council called in Moscow approved the reforms of Nikon in service books and ritual. In 1655 further regulations were published instituting a strict watch against novelties in icon painting.

The Archdeacon Paul of Aleppo, who accompanied Macarius, patriarch of Antioch, on his travels in Russia (1654-57) provides us with an eyewitness account of Nikon's attack upon "new icons drawn after the fashion of Frankish and Polish pictures." He says that Nikon ordered all newfangled icons to be collected and brought to him, even from the houses of high officials. He put out the eyes of the icons, and the *streltsy* (Tsar's musketeers) bore them round the town proclaiming that anyone who painted such icons thereafter would be severely punished. Paul further remarks: "When the Muscovites saw how the Patriarch was treating the icons, they were offended and disturbed and regarded him as an iconoclast. . . . The Patriarch anathematized and excommunicated all who should make or keep such icons. He took one icon after another in his right hand, showed it to the people and dashed it down to shatter it upon the iron floorslabs; then ordered that they should be burnt. The Tsar was standing close to us with bared head, silently listening to the sermon, but as he was very pious he quietly begged the Patriarch, 'No, Father, do not burn them. Let them be buried in the ground.' And this was done."

The movement for a return to the old ritual gathered momentum, and not all the repressive measures launched by the government could stop it. The persecution of the Old Believers by the government was ruthless, but it only heightened their fanaticism. They came to believe that the apostasy of the official church from true Orthodoxy signalized the coming of Antichrist and sought martyrdom at the hands of the triumphant Nikonians. Large groups sought sanctuary in the forests of the north and beyond the Urals. They endured unspeakable hardships, or burned themselves, locked in their churches, rather than be made to accept what seemed to them to be the ritual of the Antichrist.

The greatest figure of all among the Old Believers was the Archpriest Avvakum, fanatical, eloquent, and heroic—the most vivid and original writer and preacher of his day. A bitter opponent of religious innovation and a staunch defender of the old ritual, Avvakum refused all compromise and denounced Nikon as a heretic and a tool of Satan. He was exiled to Siberia, where he remained for nine years, dragged about from place to place and mercilessly persecuted. In 1664 he was brought back to Moscow, where considerable changes had taken place. Nikon had fallen and a Synod was to judge both Avvakum and Nikon. The Synod condemned Avvakum's tenets, and thus the Schism became final. Avvakum was exiled to Pustozerk in the far northeast of Russia. There he became an even more active and daring leader than before. He kept on preaching and writing his eloquent epistles to his followers, urging them to defy their persecutors and seek martyrdom. He himself won a martyr's crown in April, 1682; he was burned at the stake, thus inspiring among his followers a renewed passion of self-destruction before the coming of Antichrist.

The year in which the Schism began was also the year in which the Ukraine recognized the suzerainty of Muscovy. This proved to be the beginning of a succession of wars, in the course of which Muscovy's military and financial capabilities were shown to be entirely inadequate for her am-

34

bitious policies. It began to be realized in the higher echelons of the government that the country was badly in need of acquiring the military and industrial techniques and practical skills that Western Europe possessed.

Tsar Aleksei was quick to appreciate the advantages of foreign mercenaries and technicians and their value as instructors. He instituted a vigorous search for professional talent and skilled labor, which had the effect of attracting to Moscow a multitude of foreign military and technical experts, physicians, merchants, and manufacturers, thus swelling the ranks of the foreign colony and accelerating the pace of Western penetration.

Western influences invaded Moscow via two routes—one from the southwest (Poland and the Ukraine), the other from the foreign colony in the city, the so-called "German Suburb" (*Nemetskaya Sloboda*) situated northeast of the Kremlin.

Ukrainian and Polish influences gradually transformed the whole fabric of ecclesiastical civilization. In 1685 an academy on the Western model, teaching Greek and Latin, was established in Moscow. A new current of ideas and art forms entered the stream of Russian painting, architecture, literature, and music, influencing and modifying the established age-long traditions. Toward the end of the seventeenth century a whole new generation of Russian artists was reared and educated on new principles.

As a result we notice in the Russian art of that epoch two tendencies running concurrently: the old tendency prevalent in the provincial centers and the hinterland of that day, still vigorously developing the art forms bequeathed by the Moscow period; the other, the pro-Western tendency, adopting, assimilating, and refashioning the forms of the late

35

Italian Renaissance, a movement that took strong roots and became the vogue at the tsar's court and at the capital.

Even more important in its influence on Muscovite culture was the foreign colony. Chancellor had counted three hundred foreigners at Ivan the Terrible's court. Olearius, secretary to the Embassy of the Duke of Holstein (1634–38), describes the colony as comprising upwards of one thousand persons, while another foreign writer, Baron Mayerberg, who visited Moscow in 1660, speaks of a "multitude of foreigners then resident in the Foreign Quarter which contained Lutheran and Calvinist churches and a German school." In fact, the Quarter was a miniature segment of Western Europe transplanted to the northeastern outskirts of Moscow.

In Tsar Aleksei's time the most distinctly German attribute of the *Nemetskaya Sloboda* was the name, which had clung to the suburb—a reminder of the German origin of its first inhabitants. ("German" [*Nemets*] was applied in Muscovy to all the Germanic nations, including the Swedes and the English.) With the outbreak of the civil war in England and the subsequent triumph of Cromwell, several leading Scottish royalists entered Russian service. Englishmen and Scotsmen were now most prominent, and among them were noble names—Drummonds, Hamiltons, Crawfords, Leslies, and, at a later period, Gordons. In the professional class, soon to be added to this aristocratic group— among the teachers, physicians, apothecaries, traders, and artists—the dominant element was Dutch. The Dutch had a Calvinist, the Germans, two Lutheran pastors. Religious liberty reigned in the *Sloboda* except in the case of the Roman Catholics, who were forbidden to have a priest. Schools were numerous. There was a theater, frequently visited by Tsar Aleksei, where he saw a performance of *Orpheus* and was fired with the ambition of establishing a theater of his own. For the people of Moscow this settlement came to be the exponent of Western European culture. The foreign technical experts had brought with them not only their military, professional, and industrial skills, but also the amenities and conveniences of life as lived in Western Europe.

The boyar Artamon Matveev, who became head of the administration in 1669, married a Scottish lady, and was one of the first Russian nobles to set up his household on a Western scale. Through him notions of contemporary culture penetrated even to the court. Many nobles began to dress in the European fashion of the day and to trim their hair and beards. The use of snuff and of smoking tobacco was speedily acquired, much to the horror and indignation of the Orthodox, who saw in it the work of Satan.

What especially fascinated the more daring young Russian nobles in the *Sloboda* was the social life, so new to them and so different from Russian society. There was novelty and attraction in the presence of the ladies, in the ball-masquerades, and in the family feasts. Some brave souls here and there had cast off, literally and figuratively, the ancient Byzantine-Tatar garb. Western thought was quickening, new ideas were sprouting. It was the dawn of a new day.

THE CITY

Description

THE old Russian Chronicle lists Moscow among the new towns founded in the reign of the Grand Prince of Suzdal, Yuri Dolgoruky (d. 1157). It speaks of Moscow as a mere spot on the boundary line between the northern province of Suzdal and the southern province of Chernigov. At this spot, in 1147, Dolgoruky entertained his neighbor Prince Svyatoslav of Novgorod with "a mighty dinner"; and this seems to be the first mention of the name of Moscow in the Chronicle. Evidently the place was then only a country estate where the princes of Suzdal halted during their journeys to and from Kiev and where they entertained their guests.

Nine years later, the Chronicle states, Yuri "laid the town of Moskva" at a point near the confluence of the Neglinnaya and Moskva rivers, i.e., he built a wooden stockade around his estate and converted the enclosure into a fort. This fort constituted the Kremlin of Moscow in its original form, occupying the western corner of the Kremlin hill, where a steep spur runs down to the mouth of the Neglinnaya and where the Borovitskaya Tower now stands. The triangular portion of ground which Yuri fortified occupied only a third, or, at most, half of the present-day area of the Kremlin.

The word Kremlin (*Kreml'*) appears for the first time in 1331 in the report of the Moscow fire. Then for over two hundred years the word disappeared from the chronicles and historical documents. Until 1367, when the walls were still wooden, the settlement was called *gorod* (fenced-in town). When a wall was built around the adjoining settlement of Belgorod (White City) in 1589, the name *Kreml'* became permanent.

The Kremlin, the nucleus and architectural core of Moscow, is almost the exact center of the city. On the south is the Moskva River; on the east, Red Square; on the west, Alexander Park and a new, wide boulevard. From it radiate, in practically all directions, the great arterial thoroughfares of the capital. Location and historical significance make the Kremlin the very heart of Moscow.

Situated on top of a hill about 125 feet above the level of the Moskva River, the Kremlin dominates the entire city and holds within its walls all the memories and souvenirs of the city's past. Here were the See of the Orthodox faith, the palaces of the tsar, the patriarch, and the boyars, and the state, judicial, and executive offices (*prikazy*), where foreign ambassadors were received, orders issued, and justice administered. The church, the throne, the military, and the secular branches of the government—all were represented in the Kremlin by many remarkable edifices.

Strictly speaking, the outline of the Kremlin is an irregular pentagon; its sides curve slightly—concavely on the south, convexly on the east and west—and its perimeter is about a mile and a half. More broadly, except for slight irregularities, the outline of the Kremlin can be thought of as an almost equilateral triangle whose southwest angle is obtuse; the confluence of the Neglinnaya and Moskva rivers, forming the southwest vertex of the triangle, predetermined the development of its plan. On the east, facing Red Square, then a trading place, a deep moat was dug and fortified which linked the Neglinnaya River with the Moskva. Thus the Kremlin was virtually transformed into an island and became one of the strongest fortresses in the world.

The walls, flanked by towers, are arranged in straight, short lines with definite breaks. On the south side, which faces the Moskva River, the breaks are somewhat softened by a curve in the wall parallel to the almost crescent-shaped river bend. The top of the south wall is about sixty-five feet above the level of the river. Again and again, under successive shocks of war, the walls and towers have been damaged and rebuilt, but they have remained substantially unchanged in form.

The present surrounding wall is studded with nineteen towers: three massive circular towers—one at each angle of the triangle; five steepled gate towers; and eleven watchtowers and barbicans of various shapes. The interior faces of the Kremlin walls are marked by many shallow-arched niches; and there is strong reason to believe that within these thick walls are many passages, corridors, stairways, and secret chambers, only a few of which are known.

The walls are from twelve to sixteen feet thick. The ramparts, about eight feet wide with battlements on the outer side and a low parapet on the inner, are supported on filled-in arches. These parapets served as battle stations from which showers of arrows were discharged through the embrasures; later they were mounted by the musketeers, cannoneers, and their ordnance. The towers were somewhat advanced beyond the wall line so that each could be seen from the neighboring towers and all enemy activities could be closely observed.

Every tower was designed as a small fortress, independent and self-sufficient. The corner and entrance towers were considered impregnable—the enemy could penetrate them only through a narrow aperture in the roof. All the entrance towers had the additional protection of their barbicans, fronting the main gates and connected with them by drawbridges.

The walls, towers, cathedrals, and other structures had underground passages, water pipes, large vaulted cellars, and storage places for supplies. These underground passages enabled the embattled and besieged garrison to make surprise sorties and attacks or to spy on enemy activities. The underground cellars and crypts were used not only for storage of food and arms but also as a hiding place for the great treasures of the tsars.

The walls follow the topographical contours of the ground and wander up and down the hill, adding to the uniqueness and picturesqueness of the fortress. On the brow of the hill a great esplanade and the best architectural monuments of the Kremlin were developed. The Assumption, Archangel Michael, and Annunciation cathedrals, the Belfry of Ivan the Great, the white buildings with their gilt cupolas, the green declivity with the walls at the very edge of the river—all together they create an unforgettable sight.

The city of Moscow was formed around the Kremlin. Its general plan resembles somewhat that of medieval Paris; the different quarters have gradually developed around the center, and the Moskva River, about as broad and as sinuous as the Seine, washes the whole of the southern side of the Kremlin and, like the Seine, meanders through the city.

In the fourteenth and fifteenth centuries, Moscow consisted of several sections: the *Gorod* proper, that is, the walled-in Kremlin; the adjoining *Posad*, a tradesmen's and artisans' quarter east of the Kremlin (surrounded by a masonry wall in 1534–35 when it became known as Kitai-Gorod); the *Zagorodie*, the settlements beyond the Kremlin, extending northwest of the Neglinnaya River; and the *Zarechye*, the settlement on the south side of the Moskva River. As in most medieval Russian cities, these settlements were grouped around the citadel, forming a series of concentric belts. A number of arterial roads led toward the center from neighboring cities, provinces, and principalities. With the growth of the city these old roads became the principal city streets. Thus in present-day Moscow, Gertsen Street (Hertsen, formerly Nikitskaya) was originally the main highway to Novgorod; Gorky Street (formerly Tverskaya) was the highway to Tver. Sretenka led to Yaroslavl, and Prechistenka was the old road to Smolensk.

East of the Kremlin walls swirled the life of Kitai-Gorod, whose main part, called "*Bolshoi Posad*," was located northeast of the Kremlin stretching about as far as the Sretensky Monastery (near the present Sretenskie Gates) and the lower reaches of the Yauza River. Kitai-Gorod with its central market and inns for visiting and foreign merchants was the busiest, most crowded, and richest section of the city. Its name is derived from the woven baskets, known as *Kit* or *Kita*, which, filled with earth, were used like gabions to reinforce the wall. (Kitai-Gorod has been at times erroneously translated as Chinatown, *Kitai* being the modern Russian word for China.) The steep right bank of the Neglinnaya River was also built up. However, the area was not solidly covered with structures. There were empty spaces where the all too frequent fires had consumed many build-

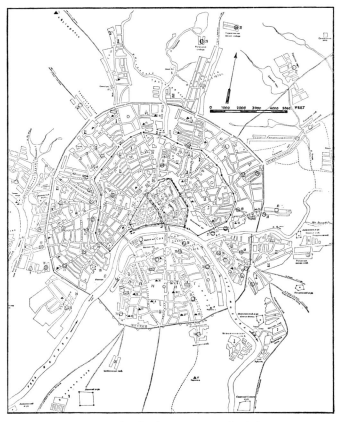

From a drawing by S. K. Bogoyavlensky
in *Istoriia Moskvy*, edited by I. A. Golublsov

Moscow about the middle of the seventeenth century. The Kremlin and adjoining Kitai-Gorod (to the right) are in the very center of the ringed-in city.

ings. Besides, many princes, boyars, and rich merchants had extensive farms and orchards in the *Posad*.

In the sixteenth century, on the northern and eastern boundaries of the Kremlin and Kitai-Gorod, a number of settlements and streets were developed which jointly came to be known as Belgorod (White City). This horseshoe-shaped district surrounded the northern, eastern, and western boundaries of the combined territories of the Kremlin and Kitai-Gorod.

The necessity of protecting the new district from repeated raids and devastation by the Crimean Tatars prompted the Moscow government to fortify it; and thus, after the death of Ivan IV, a white stone wall, nine kilometers long, with twenty-eight towers, was erected, enclosing the settlement beyond Kitai-Gorod. Gates were cut in the wall where highways from neighboring towns to Kitai-Gorod crossed it. The present boulevards follow the line of this wall.

Finally, a wooden wall, subsequently replaced by an earthen rampart, was constructed in 1591 along the route which is at present known as the Sadovoe Ring (*Sadovoe Koltso*)—forming a circular enclosure of sixteenth-century Moscow and its suburbs. This earthen rampart gave its name to Moscow's outer belt, which became known as Zemlyanoy Gorod (Earthen City), also known as Skorodom. It constituted Moscow's last outer line of defenses—enclosing the Simonov, Donskoy, and Danilov fortress-monasteries and the fortified Novodevichei Convent and covering the approaches to Moscow from the south. The Zemlyanoy Gorod was inhabited chiefly by craftsmen who lived in their respective districts. The districts of coach drivers, dealers in sheepskins, gardeners, and weavers and a few musketeer districts were located on the south side of the Moskva River.

According to foreign visitors, Moscow at the beginning of the sixteenth century was as large as the biggest cities in Western Europe. To them the city seemed larger than London and Prague. The houses, mainly of wood, were surrounded by large gardens and outbuildings, and many open spaces were left to act as firebreaks. It was natural that the European visitor, accustomed to the masonry-built and compact cities of the West, would get the impression of great size. Archdeacon William Coxe found the streets of Moscow to be "exceedingly long and broad," and early seventeenth-century maps and views show an orderly alignment along the curving streets. The Kremlin and the city contained many substantial masonry structures. The real beauty and glory of Moscow were her Kremlin, her churches and monasteries. The many churches, with their gleaming cupolas and white walls, were freely scattered among the wood houses. Six fortified monasteries and convents—the Andronikov, Novospasky, Simonov, Danilov, Donskoy, and Novodevichei—encircled Moscow like a necklace. These fortified monasteries were the most characteristic feature of the Moscow architectural landscape. They symbolized the political and economical importance of the black (monastic) clergy and were quite effective militarily. They were the Muscovite equivalent of the secular castles of Europe.

The Kremlin represented splendor and magnificence: buildings of white stone, brick, varicolored tiles, and shining metals. Surrounded on all sides by walls, rivers, and a moat, it had the appearance of a powerful and picturesque fortress. A prodigious stage *décor* with reds and golds predominating, painted against the background of the sky, the Kremlin remains an exuberant expression of polychrome decorative architecture of essentially Russian elements: bulbous cupolas clad in gold and silver; octagonal or square towers giving rise to other towers surmounted by lanterns and slender, tent-shaped pinnacles; bright multicolored roofs producing the effect of enamel inlay; belfries and watchtowers, ramparts, and machicolated battlements; everywhere and above all, imposing on this decorative ensemble a sense of unity and domination, is the obstinate repetition of the Russian bulb motif scintillating in the air like so many balls of fire.

The city conformed to no strict building plan, despite the fact that the Kremlin and the principal monasteries formed focal points. The center of Moscow grew up in a rough approximation to a spider's web, with two inner ring roads on the sites of old fortifications. All around the city lay manors and estates belonging for the most part to the tsar, the great boyars, and the church. The city with its mansions, hovels, shops, markets, and all its busy trade overflowed into suburbs—some open, some protected by wooden stockades—stretching out into the country, where meadows and tilled fields mingled with the houses and shops. Industrial activities were scattered still farther afield in spacious *faubourgs* and hamlets surrounded by woods, gardens, and orchards, with more monasteries, whose white masonry walls and gilded church cupolas carried the landscape, half-urban, half-rustic, far out to the horizon.

From a distance, Moscow, immersed in greenery and gleaming with its hundreds of golden cupolas, seemed a fascinating city, but its charm vanished when the traveler entered its depressingly dirty and muddy streets.

Population

The population of mid-seventeenth-century Moscow is

difficult to estimate, since precise information is lacking. But a fair guess, according to Professor S. K. Bogoyavlensky, would be about 200,000. The bulk of the lower-class civilian population consisted of tradesmen and artisans who were divided into three groups: the tax-bound townspeople proper, burghers, such as retail merchants and master craftsmen, who paid their taxes either in cash or in kind; a considerable group of craftsmen, artisans, and unskilled laborers who worked for the tsar's court and various government departments; and dependents of private property owners, on whose land they worked and lived.

The workers of every individual trade were organized into guilds or trade associations. They lived and worked in the so-called "Black Settlements" (*Chernyie Slobody*) and "Black Hundreds" Settlements (*Chernyie Sotni*). In modern Russian the word *Sloboda* (*Slobody*, pl.)—a corruption of *Svoboda*—means liberty, but in the pre-Petrine period it meant a special city district, quarter, or settlement; the words *Chernyie Slobody* meant districts or settlements whose inhabitants were subject to taxation; the word *sotnya* (*sotni*, pl.) meant both a given trade unit and the district or the quarter where the particular tradesmen or artisans lived and worked. The districts and quarters were under the jurisdiction of the Land Chancellory which had a special department dealing with their affairs.

Bogoyavlensky lists nine Black *Sotni* Districts, twelve Black *Slobody*, and fifty Crown or Court *Slobody*. In addition, there were a considerable number of *Slobody* belonging to some of the great boyars and the patriarch. The latter owned large establishments in the Kremlin, in Kitai-Gorod, Zaradye, and seven *Slobody* in various parts of Moscow. Of the military there were thirty-seven *Slobody*. According to

Bogoyavlensky's figures the various Black Districts, including those that worked for the tsar's court, contained about 48,000 people; other parts of the city contained 53,000 members of the boyardom and the lesser nobility, including their retainers and serfs; 27,000 members of the clergy; 44,000 of the military; and 28,000 foreigners.

The Moscow boyardom consisted of varied and heterogeneous elements. Some of the older noble families were originally of Norse extraction; those of the fourteenth and fifteenth centuries belonged to the old boyar families of the Vladimir Principality. Among the most notable of the Moscow boyars may be cited the Romanovs, the Morozovs, the Buturlins, the Chelyadnins, the Velyaminovs, the Vorontsovs, the Khovrins, the Golovins, the Godunovs, and the Saburovs.

The Orthodox clergy was divided into two sections: the white (secular) and black (monastic). Each had its own peculiarities and special privileges. Clergymen were immune from civil jurisdiction and neither served nor paid taxes. They were not the tsar's serfs, but his "supplicants before God." The abbots and bishops of the great monasteries, besides being a dominant social and economic force as the possessors of about one-third of all the land, were the guardians of the national theocratic tradition and the highest spiritual authority in the country. During the national assemblies the clergy took precedence over the boyars and secular delegates. The black clergy, as a whole, was a major feudal force which rapidly amassed extensive land holdings and great economic wealth. High-ranking members of the black clergy, the abbots and bishops, were prominent in politics and cultural undertakings. The upper layer of the white clergy, the priests of the great city churches, were as highly

48

educated as the bishops and abbots. In life and outlook they were closely connected with the commercial class, and their social influence was considerable. One of the body, the Archpriest Sylvester, was the head of Ivan IV's most brilliant and progressive administration in the middle of the sixteenth century.

The top layer of the Muscovite merchants, the *gosti* and *sukonniki*, were a privileged minority high above the bulk of the townspeople. In the sixteenth century that top layer was divided into three groups: the *gosti*, the richest wholesale merchants; the *gosti* hundred (*gostinnaya sotnya*), a corporation of the less important merchants; and the *sukonniki* hundred (*sukonnaya sotnya*), the corporation of the merchants dealing in textiles. All of them were exempt from direct taxation as well as from any compulsory labor services. The *gosti* were employed in the tsar's financial service; though they bore a heavy responsibility, they had ample opportunities for increasing their fortunes.

Moscow had a large garrison consisting of cavalry, artillery, and infantry. Special units manned the fortification posts; others were assigned to guard duty at the various city gates. There was a special Royal Bodyguard unit which numbered one thousand men in the time of Ivan the Terrible and seven thousand by the end of the seventeenth century. This was a body of elite well-equipped troops dressed in colorful uniforms, and in the words of Richard Chancellor, "Their sumptuousness was above measure, not only in themselves, but also in their horses, as velvet, cloth of gold, and cloth of silver set with pearles and not scant."

The infantry was largely represented by the *streltsy* (musketeers) regiments. They were first organized by Ivan the Terrible, and they constituted the most efficient part of the army until the importation of foreign officers and military advisers was begun under Tsar Mikhail Romanov. The number of *streltsy* stationed in Moscow varied from time to time, as some units were often shifted to the provincial cities; others were assigned to convoy and police duties, often to suppress the frequent uprisings in the capital and the provinces. The 1681 census listed 22,452 *streltsy* living with their families in specially designated *slobody* strategically distributed all over Moscow, most of them located around the fortifications of the Kremlin and Kitai-Gorod. They formed a distinct class, socially inferior to, but not worse off than the lesser ranks of the nobility; for besides their pay they were granted immunity from taxes and custom duties, were free to engage in petty trade and various industrial activities, and were provided with cloth for their uniforms—each regiment having its own special color: green, red, blue, and cherry. In the seventeenth century they were among the most reactionary elements in the country. They were especially opposed to the army reforms and to the tide of Westernization and often attempted to act highhandedly as champions of the old order and even to intervene in state administrative matters. The most serious *streltsy* revolts occurred in 1682 and 1698 and led to wholesale executions by Peter I in 1699.

In this large city of 200,000 people the streets were filled with the most varied collection of humanity imaginable. Aside from foreign visitors, the residents of Moscow were themselves of mixed origin. Most people showed a mixture of blood from all the western and eastern states which the Muscovite tsardom had absorbed, each with its own language or dialect and its own culture and traditions. There were

Tatars descended from the Mongol races; nationals from the Middle East, the Balkan and Mediterranean countries; Greeks, Bulgarians, Serbians, Italians (Genoese and Venetian), Armenians, Lithuanians, Poles, and Germans.

The Greek colony was fairly large and had its own monastery near the Kremlin. Relations between Constantinople and Moscow in the fourteenth and fifteenth centuries were much closer than in later years, and Greek influence was instrumental in bringing metropolitans and bishops from Byzantium to Moscow. Such church prelates as Theognostus and Photius mantained large staffs of Greek assistants. The center of Byzantine enlightenment in Moscow was the Bogoyavlensky Monastery, whose monks were in close touch with the Metropolitan Theognostus, himself a Greek. As mentioncd earlier, one of these monks, Aleksei, became metropolitan of Moscow, and it was he who was instrumental in establishing other Moscow centers of Byzantine education—the Simonov, Andronikov, and Chudov monasteries. In the seventeenth century the Greek community grew large enough to occupy its own *sloboda*, located in the Transyauza Region.

Among the other foreigners who lived in Moscow were Italians or, as they were known in those days, *Friazins*, a name applied to all Latins of the Mediterranean Basin. Close relations between Russians and Italians were not encouraged by the Russian church because of the fear of Latin infection. At the end of the fifteenth century, Moscow had a considerable number of Italians, consisting mostly of jewelers, coinminting specialists, and masonry fortification builders.

An important element in the Moscow population were the Tatars and other peoples of the Mussulman faith. Most of them were traders and lived in the Tatar *sloboda* located in the Zarechye Region. A number of present-day streets, the Balchuga and the Ordynka, still carry Tatar names.

New blood was constantly coming in from outside Muscovy. Mercenary soldiers made up a large part of the army command. Germans in considerable numbers were employed by Ivan the Terrible; French, Swedes, Scots—all were attracted by the armed service and often settled in Moscow when they retired.

The old foreign colony founded at Moscow by Ivan the Terrible, though scattered during the Time of Trouble, was soon repopulated with foreign professional men, technicians, merchants, and artisans. The colony, made up mostly of Protestant immigrants, was first situated near the Kremlin. After 1613, the accession of the first Romanov, Tsar Mikhail, the influx of foreigners to the capital increased, and newcomers settled wherever they could and built their own churches, schools, and breweries within the walls of Moscow itself. It began to seem to the Russian religious zealots that their "holy city" was being profaned by the customs and the heretical ideas of foreigners, and an edict was issued forbidding foreigners to acquire property from the natives or to build their churches within the walls of Moscow. A site was granted for a new church beyond the Zemlyanoy Gorod, and the many foreigners scattered throughout the city were evicted from the capital and settled in the new foreign quarter on the banks of the Yauza River, where, according to status, professions, and trades, they were allotted plots of land. The new settlement quickly developed into a large and well-built suburb with straight, broad avenues, squares, and fountains. By the end of the seventeenth century this suburb was one-fifth the total size of the capital. It looked more like a European town than a suburb of Moscow. In startling contrast to the crowded conditions of Moscow, everything here was laid out in order. The palaces and larger houses were entirely in the European manner: two- and three-storied brick or wood mansions with large windows, and decorated with columns, pilasters, and cornices; even the grounds were arranged as European flower gardens with pavilions and pools. It was here that Peter the Great was introduced to European architecture and the purely material achievements of European civilization; here he built the mansions for his collaborators and favorites; and it was probably here that the idea of building a new capital was born.

Industrial and Commercial Activities

In the seventeenth century the economic development of Moscow entered a new phase, and the city became the most important industrial and trading center in the country. It had large contingents of craftsmen and artisans who produced and sold food products, building materials, leather articles, textiles, arms, armor, icons, manuscripts, jewelry, and other luxury goods. According to their trade specialties and techniques, these craftsmen and artisans lived and conducted their business in the same part of the city or on the same street. The names of certain districts and streets which have been preserved to this day are a reminder of those activities; for example, Khlebny (Bread), Kalachny (Fancy Bread Loafs), Bronnaya (Armor), Khamovnicheskaya (Weavers), Granatny (Grenade), and so on.

The capital attracted the best craftsmen of the land and provided favorable conditions for production and sale of articles requiring artistry and skill. The contacts with provincial and foreign craftsmanship which only a great metropolis could offer were of inestimable value, for they brought familiarity with the skills and techniques of diverse peoples, thus stimulating competition and introducing innovations in design and perfection of craftsmanship.

The crafts were divided into specialties. For instance, the clothing craftsmen were divided into sheepskin coat tailors, hatters, *sarafan* makers, pants and jacket bushelmen, and so on. Particularly were there many specialties in the food industry: pancake makers, pastry bakers, kvas brewers, jelly and jam makers, confectioners, and biscuit bakers. All told, there were about 250 different crafts in Moscow. Here were produced various goods for the city's consumption and for export as well.

Icon painting was a flourishing industry. The great majority of the painters came from monasteries or from the parochial clergy. There were a number of Moscow metropolitans (Peter, Simon, Varlaam, and Makari) who gained fame as icon painters. But the very nature of the work—its technique and materials—required the participation of many lay artists, craftsmen, and artisans drawn from the common townspeople. In the seventeenth century there existed in the Moscow Arbat Region a special Iconographers Quarter and a church dedicated to St. Luke, who by tradition was considered to be the first icon painter.

The city was a major center of metalworking. The census of 1641 listed sixty-nine smithies in the Earthen City, thirty-five in the White City, twenty-nine in the district south of the Moskva River, and nineteen in various other parts of Moscow. The demand for fine blacksmith work was at its height during the intensive building activities of the seventeenth century. The production of metal objects was significantly increased when ironworks were established near

Moscow and Tula, thus making metal products at reason-
able prices available to the public. Since the city had been
plagued with frequent fires and night robberies, **buildings**
were often provided with heavy metal gates and grilles, solid
metal doors, and window shutters. The early ironwork of
Moscow was extremely simple, such as plain round or square
bars, sometimes pierced, with almost no molded work. It was
peculiarly suited to the character of Russian seventeenth-
century design, and its popularity brought forth a great
many fine examples, the most notable being the gateway to
the western portal of the Nikitinskaya Church in Moscow.
Although the churches contain the best existing ironwork,
there were many fine examples in the palaces of the rich and
the houses of the lowly. Candlesticks, lamp brackets, torch
holders, and braziers were designed and executed with fine
understanding of the material. The craft of the blacksmith
also found its application in the production of hardware,
i.e., all that metalwork which operates, decorates, or secures
doors, gates, and other hinged barriers. Hinges and straps,
locks, drop and lever handles, bolts, knobs, and latches were
produced by a variety of methods. There were many other
articles which the blacksmith provided, such as church
crosses, church chandeliers, heraldic eagles, weather vanes,
and signs. The pliability, freedom, and refinement possible
to forged iron were skillfully utilized by the Moscow
craftsmen.

The production of firearms in Moscow dates from the last
quarter of the fourteenth century. General V. G. Fedorov,
in his well-documented book on the subject, asserts that, in
addition to arrows, short-range heavy buckshot guns were
used by the Muscovites during the Tatar siege in 1382. The
manufacture of cannon was greatly intensified at the end of

the fifteenth century, when major technical improvements were made in casting. Moscow became a major arsenal providing firearms and ammunition for all of sixteenth-century Russia. The main plant was located in the center of the city on the banks of the Neglinnaya River. It was at this plant, during the reign of Ivan IV, that the celebrated metal-casting craftsman Andrei Chokhov worked. He is credited with the production of more than sixteen hundred cannons, the most famous of which is the so-called "King of Cannon" (*Tsar Pushka*) now in the Kremlin, weighing about forty tons. Designed by Chokhov in 1586 at the command of Tsar Feodor, this gargantuan piece of artillery has never served any but a purely decorative function. Tsar Feodor's equestrian portrait, surrounded by rich ornamentation in relief, appears upon it.

The Moscow armorers (*bronniki*) were skilled in the intricate techniques of producing helmets, coats of mail, and parade armor. Most of them were employed in the Kremlin Armory (Oruzheinaya Palata). They lived in a special district which in the seventeenth century was located in the region of the present Tver Boulevard.

The production of copper and bronze articles was centered in the Kotelnaya District of the Transyauza Region. The census of 1638 lists sixty coppersmiths engaged in the production of copper and brass articles for use by the church and the community at large. Among the best known of these craftsmen was Dmitri Sverchkov, who designed and executed in 1625 the Repository of the Robe of Our Lord and the dias above the main altar in the Assumption Cathedral in the Kremlin. The craft of the coppersmith also found its application in the production of cooking utensils, chandeliers, caskets, crosses, reliquaries, and grilles; the most famous of the last is the so-called "Golden Grille" in the Terem Palace of the Kremlin. It was cast in 1670 from the copper coins minted in 1662 to replace silver. The copper coins caused a financial panic and brought about a bloody uprising (the copper revolt), killing about seven thousand people.

In general, what is noteworthy in that period is the fine workmanship and mechanical perfection. The tools and equipment were few and simple, but the craftsmen made good use of them and displayed great skill and ingenuity in producing highly complicated and artistic objects without the aid of machines. Their main talent was the resourcefulness and dexterity with which they handled the embossing and chasing tools. Using a simple hammer, anvil, and wooden bench, they were able to produce large reliefs of sharp convexity as well as the most elegant and delicate designs: flowers, fruit, human and animal figures arranged with taste, symmetry, and balance on subtly wrought backgrounds.

The manufacture of tiles and the art of glazing and coloring them, known in Muscovite Russia as *tseninnoe delo* was a flourishing industry. The tileworks and its craftsmen were located in the Transyauza Pottery District. The initiative in developing this craft must be credited to Patriarch Nikon, under whom much was done in this field, first at the Iverski Valdaiski Monastery (founded by him in 1653), and then (1656), on a much larger scale, at his new enterprise, the New Jerusalem Resurrection Monastery near Moscow. The exterior and interior tile ornamentation in the principal church of the monastery is a rare example of seventeenth-century Moscow decorative art. Another favorite application of faïence tile was in the decoration of heating stoves. There are many fine examples in the apartments of the *terems* of the Kremlin and in various monasteries and churches. These stoves are rectangular or circular and often resemble minia-ture storied buildings complete with bases, niches, arches, columns, and cornices. Most of them are decorated with amusing allegorical designs and bands or friezes carrying humorous mottoes.

The carpenters and cabinetmakers lived and worked in the region now known as the Pokrovskiye Gates. Beyond these gates was located the famous wood market displaying prefabricated lumber, tenoned and mortised timbers of lengths suitable for houses of various sizes—indispensable to a population which suffered from frequent devastating fires. The buyer would specify the number of rooms, examine the timbers and other parts of the structure, all clearly marked and numbered for assembly, bargain with the vendor, and have the lumber delivered. A house thus could be bought, transported, and erected within a few days.

Seventeenth-century Moscow craftsmen attained great skill in many media, and her designers developed a number of patterns based on a few traditional national themes which were remarkably viable and prolific. The variety of skilled crafts, including those of an artistic nature, was instrumental in forming the nuclei of the post-Petrine contingents of skilled labor and craftsmen. The intense working regime of Moscow life produced many capable experienced hands and so greatly contributed to the fast development of the new eighteenth-century manufacturing enterprises.

Moscow's exceptionally favorable geographical position contributed much to the development of domestic trade. Agricultural products came from the south; fish in large quantities and varieties came from various regions, especially the lower Volga; meat from the northern provinces; hides from Kazan; furs from the Siberian taiga; and metals from Tula and the Urals. The major production centers of the land sent their best wares to the Moscow market: Yaroslavl, Veliki Ustiug, Tula, and Kholmogory furnished metal products; Tver, Kostroma, Yaroslavl, and Vologda provided linens; Nizhny Novgorod supplied wood products; enamels came from Kiev and Solvychegodsk; bone carvings from Kholmogory, Archangel, and Tobolsk.

Moscow was the focus of three groups of water routes: the western group to Northern Europe via the Baltic, the Volga Middle East route with its trading centers on the lower Volga and the Caspian, and the northeastern routes to Siberia. The last supplied the precious furs which have produced so much foreign revenue for Russia. The first two routes, which together constituted a basic transit route from Northern Europe to Persia, connected Moscow with the world market; and Moscow became an important factor in the rapidly developing European commercial revolution, especially after the English discovered the White Sea route to Russia in 1553. Since Moscow was the largest trade transit center between Western Europe and the countries of the East, England, Denmark, Holland, and Sweden were most interested in the development of trade with Russia. Although the Muscovite government was anxious to expand commerce with foreign states, its chief aim was to encourage home trade. More and more the city drew the trading within the country to herself, and at the same time kept on expanding her commerce with distant lands. Her principal exports during this period were furs: fine Pechora sables, beavers, silver foxes, martens, ermine, and squirrels; other exports were timber, hemp, pitch, wax, grain, honey, fats, and other commodities. The chief imports were manufactured articles, arms, and luxury goods. In the middle of the seventeenth century, spurred by the demands of the Moscow merchants, the government abolished the special privileges enjoyed by the English, Dutch, Swedish, and other foreign merchants. The foreigners were also deprived of the right to engage in retail trade. The new trading regulation of 1667 granted Moscow merchants a monopoly of transit trade.

CHAPTER THREE

DAILY LIFE

N EARLY every phase of daily life in Moscow was colored with religious sentiment and usage, and the church canons were considered to be as binding on each citizen as were the laws of the state. Churches, chapels, and shrines were numerous and well attended. Time and space were both full of saints; every parishioner and every trade or occupation had its patron saint. Many institutions—secular and ecclesiastical—were named after saints, and not only their birthdays and martyrdom days were celebrated but also the days when their relics had been discovered or brought to some church for enshrinement. Days were counted by the ecclesiastical calendar; hours, by the time of divine services.

Moscow rose early. At dawn or before, the city would be awakened by the sound of church bells summoning the people to early church service. Every morning would begin with the ringing of bells, repeated many times during the day. They rang for festivals, fasts, and fires; for marriages and funerals; and they rang for work to begin and for work to cease.

The Muscovites have always had a fondness for bells; at the end of the sixteenth century they seem to have been regarded as sacred instruments of worship. The bells were cast in copper and silver in many sizes and every possible variety of timbre, power, and beauty of sound. Infinite tone-color effects were created by the various choirs of bells giving utterance to religious and lay emotions. On days of disaster or funerals, certain bells were tolled; on days commemorating some happy event, other bells were used; on holidays or days of celebration, all the bells went into action. The first stroke was usually sounded from the Bono Belfry in the Kremlin (which houses the largest bell) and then taken up by bells of the Tower of Ivan Veliky, followed by all the bells of the "forty-forties" (*sorok-sorokov*) of churches in Moscow, booming and rolling in unison over the city like the waves of the sea or ringing out singly in soft resonance like a song of meditation. The city lived with this incessant chiming of bells, however much it annoyed foreign visitors.

Foreigners, including the Orthodox Greeks, were astonished at the length and magnificence of the Russian church services and the austerity of the fasts, which were as strictly observed by the tsar and the boyars as by the simple peasants. Many of the Greek visitors stated that to live among such hardy people was almost equivalent to suicide, for no one except the Russians could remain standing for such long hours at church services and remain almost without food during the seven weeks of Lent.

The Archdeacon Paul of Aleppo, after having witnessed a service lasting from 8:00 A.M. to 3:00 P.M., exclaimed: "Now what shall we say to these duties, severe enough to turn children's hair gray, so strictly observed by the tsar, tsaritsa, patriarch, boyars and their wives, standing upright from morning till evening? Who would believe that they should thus go beyond the devout anchorites of the desert?"

Lent, according to Sigismund von Herberstein, ambassador from Vienna to the court of Grand Prince Vasili III, was observed in the following manner: "They fast seven whole weeks in lent. In the first week they use milk products which they call *syrnaia*, cheese-like substances. Indeed during the following weeks all (excepting travelers) also abstain from fish. Some who eat food on Sundays and Saturdays abstain from all foods on the other days. There are those who eat food on Sundays, Tuesdays, Thursdays, and Saturdays, and abstain the other three days. Also many can be found who are content when a piece of bread has been eaten with water on Mondays, Wednesdays, and Fridays."

The Muscovite ideal of piety, morality, and a proper life pattern was outwardly exemplified at the tsar's court, among the boyars, the higher government functionaries, the white clergy, and the upper layer of the commercial class. The most complete expression of the stately decorum of every moment of life was reflected in the elaborate ritual that surrounded the tsar, especially at the courts of Feodor I, Boris Godunov, and Mikhail and Aleksei Romanov. Among the classes that best preserved the Muscovite ideal were the merchants.

The family was strictly patriarchal and subject to the absolute authority of the head of the house. Among the upper classes, including the merchants, it was isolated and self-contained. The routine of family life was determined by a code of regulations embodied in the *Domostroy*, a book aimed at regimenting human behavior to the smallest detail and providing a religious, political, moral, and practical life pattern for the family under the guidance of the father and husband. The *Domostroy* exercised a strong influence on the customs of the land for generations and was instrumental in excluding women from public life, relegating them to separate quarters in the house, the *terem*.

The Western European chivalrous cult was conspicuously absent in Moscow. The relation of the sexes might assume only one of two forms—patriarchal marriage or gross carnal intercourse. Mixed company was as rigorously excluded from Muscovite as from Mohammedan life, and men's company, even among the upper classes, as soon as liquor appeared, was inclined to lose all semblance of propriety. Men met and conversed before and after the long church services, at banquets, on hunting expeditions, and at other social events that made up their lives; they were not much in the company of the women. The Russian woman lived in her *terem,* where life was kept quiet and dull. In contrast, male society was turbulent, with its braggadocio and trials of strength, habitually degenerating into drunkenness and debauchery.

Not least among the causes of this were the separation of the sexes and the submissiveness of the Russian woman. Widows and unmarried princesses might, now and then, have a life of their own and show energy and initiative. More than one of the grand princes' widows endeavored, often with success, to assert the sovereignty and heritage of her sons. There were women who defiantly went through unspeakable tortures for days on end for the sake of their religious convictions. (The best known of them is Boyarina Morozova—the subject of Vasili Surikov's famous painting.) But most Muscovite women knew very little of these things. They kept silent when men were talking, were gentle and docile, and allowed their marriages to be arranged for them with a view to serving the family prestige and aspirations which their social position demanded.

The Muscovite woman was secluded in her *terem* and subordinated to the patriarchal rule of her husband. On the other
hand, her economic independence towards the end of the
Muscovite period became complete. The Code of 1649 established the principle that a woman's property rights were not
affected by marriage; it also stressed the complete separation
of property between husband and wife. Only in the lower
classes, where there was no property to keep separate, did
woman become the complete subject of her husband.

There was a side to Muscovite life that was coarse and
crude, and many practices were disgusting and revolting to
European visitors. Most Western accounts of Muscovy are
far from flattering, owing in part to political hostility and
to the profound incompatibility of the Puritan and Muscovite standpoints, but also to the fact that even judged by its
own standards Muscovite behavior fell short of the ideal.
Early twentieth-century Russian historians S. K. Bogoyavlensky, V. V. Nechaev, Ivan Zabelin, and others dwell at
length on this seamy side of seventeenth-century life in
Moscow. Its crudity was largely due to the very low standard
of life among the masses.

What struck the foreign observer most was the coarse,
abusive language used by the Muscovites—its raciness and
gross obscenity. Olearius—one of the keenest foreign observers of seventeenth-century Moscow life—writes: "They
[the Russians] are, in general, the most quarrelsome people,
and they upbraid each other with outrageously indecent
words: one can often observe such quarrels and wrangles
on the streets and squares, and they are carried on so heatedly
and acrimoniously, one would think they would seize each
other by the hair. However, these rows rarely culminate in

physical violence, and, if it does come to that, it usually takes the form of a fist fight." This simple method of settling a quarrel and of obtaining satisfaction for an insult was commonly used by both the upper and lower classes.

The use of coarse invective, bloodcurdling oaths, and richly embroidered five-letter words (the Russian equivalent of the English four-letter words) was common. In noting this peculiarity of the Russian conversational language, foreign observers unanimously described it as "disgusting and shameful." Olearius asserts that the government did make an effort to eradicate the public use of coarse language. Profanity and obscene language were forbidden on pain of public flogging administered on the spot. "However," remarks Olearius, "this very old and deeply ingrained habit of using profanity was beyond the control of the authorities, as the use of it was habitual among the highly placed, as well as among the lowly, and the very officials who were called upon to apprehend and punish the offenders."

An illuminating case in point is an incident related by Paul of Aleppo: "Tsar Aleksei Mikhailovich and the Patriarch of Antioch were both present at the early Mass in the Savin Monastery. When the officiating deacon, on beginning to read the chapter from the life of the calendar saint, turned toward the Patriarch and intoned: 'Bless us O Father.' The Tsar got up from his throne and yelled: 'What are you saying, you *muzhik* [peasant], son of a whore, the Patriarch is here—say "Bless us O Lord"!' "

This widespread use of profanity was only one of the manifestations of moral laxity observed in both private and public life. Foreigners were at a loss to find adjectives strong enough to describe the total lack of shame of the Muscovites.

One of the most striking examples of utter shamelessness observed by Olearius on the streets of Moscow was the frequent appearance of stark-naked women in front of the public baths, disporting themselves in the open. While cooling off after leaving the steaming bath chambers—an old-established Russian custom—these women would approach the gaping foreigners without the slightest sign of embarrassment and address them "in immoral language."

In general, Western European visitors were often shocked by some of the Moscow street scenes, and nearly all of them stressed the unusual propensity of the Muscovites for carnal pleasures. Although prostitution was not officially tolerated in Moscow, the contingent of prostitutes, both professional and casual, was always sizable. Debauchery and perversion were rampant. The startling manifestations of moral dissoluteness were conspicuously connected with one of the most evident national characteristics, drunkenness.

Much had been said and written about Russia's inebriety. Apparently, the Russian, from times immemorial, has shown a marked fondness for hard liquor. Characteristically, it was consumed without moderation, so it is not surprising that the drinking bouts were usually followed by debauchery. According to Olearius no Russian would ever willingly miss a chance to have a drink, no matter where or under what circumstances. If a person of quality invited a commoner to drink, the latter felt that he could not possibly refuse for fear of insulting his host, no matter how many drinks he was given; he would continue downing them one after another until he became utterly unconscious and hit the floor—in some cases drop dead. The same was true of the upper classes. Even the tsar's ambassadors to foreign lands never knew when to stop, and they were always eager to see their counterparts—the foreign envoys to the Russian court—as drunk as possible.

Herberstein gives us a vivid description of the drinking customs of the prince's courtiers and their manner of proposing toasts: "Silver goblets and various other vessels containing liquor are produced, and all strive to make each other drunk; and very clever they are in finding excuses for inviting men to drink, and when they are at a loss for a toast to propose, they begin at last to drink to the health of the emperor and the prince, his brother, and after that to the welfare of any others whom they believe to hold any position of dignity and honor. They think that no one ought or can refuse the cup when these names are proposed. The drinking is done in this fashion. He who proposes the toast takes his cup and goes into the middle of the room, and standing with his head uncovered, pronounces in a festive speech the name of him whose health he wishes to drink, and what he has to say in his behalf. Then after emptying the cup, he turns it upside down over his head, so that all may see that he has emptied it, and that he sincerely gave the health of the person in honor of whom the toast was drunk. He then goes to the top of the table and orders many cups to be filled, and then hands each man his cup, pronouncing the name of the party whose health is to be drunk, on which each is obliged to go into the middle of the room, and, after emptying his cup, to return to his place. He who wishes to escape too long a drinking bout must pretend that he is drunk or asleep, or at least declare that, having already emptied many cups, he cannot drink any more; for they do not think that their guests are well received, or hospitably treated, unless they are sent home drunk." Olearius states that nobody seemed to pay any attention to people lying dead-drunk in the filthy street gutters; occasionally a passing cab driver, on recognizing an acquaintance among the drunk, would pick him up, deliver him home, and collect the fare.

Although drunkenness was a common sight on the streets of Moscow, especially on Sundays and holidays, it was less common on weekdays, for not every commoner was able to obtain hard liquor at will. The sale of vodka, beginning from the sixteenth century when this drink appeared for the first time in Russia, was a monopoly of the government. However, the government was not able to take over the liquor business entirely; it had to share tavern rights with the upper clergy, the monasteries, and the boyars. The first Russian tavern (*kabak*) was founded by Ivan the Terrible in 1552, and from that time on the number of taverns grew very rapidly, spreading all over Moscow. These were the kind of public houses where one could obtain any amount of vodka. If the customer had no money, he could pawn any valuables he happened to have or hand over to the barkeeper his clothes piece by piece, very often literally stripping himself. The *kabak* was also the usual den where all kinds of shady characters—cardsharks, thieves, and robbers—hung around, always on the lookout for easy prey. The steady increase in the number of these taverns continued until 1652, when the government closed them everywhere and concentrated the sale of vodka in specially designated stores, called *kruzhalo,* only one of which was allotted to each city. The *kruzhalo* served as a liquor storehouse or depot, selling vodka retail, but sales were usually made in definite, more or less sizable quantities—by the *kruzhka* (mug) or by the *vedro* (a bucket containing twenty-one pints). Having an almost exclusive monopoly on the liquor market, the government could at will regulate the consumption of vodka by reducing the number of days on which selling of liquor was permitted. During the first half of the sixteenth century, the common people were permitted to drink only on major holidays, of which, in those days, there were not many: Christmas, Easter, Holy Trinity Day, and a few others. On Sundays and on minor church holidays people went to work after morning services. Up to the publication of the Code of Laws (*Ulozhenie*) in 1649, Sunday was considered a working day. When the new law made Sunday an obligatory holiday, the incidence of drunkenness greatly increased. In 1652, the government, having instituted the liquor storehouses, forbade the sale of liquor on fast days. These storehouses would be closed during Easter week from Sunday to Wednesday. A drunk caught during fast days faced punishment by the knout and prison.

These prohibitory measures were of no great help in reducing drunkenness. True, one person desiring to get drunk could not obtain a large quantity of liquor at will, but there were ways of circumventing the official regulations. The fact was that, while the government had the monopoly of selling vodka, it was unable to monopolize its manufacture. The right to distill liquor belonged not only to the clergy and the boyars but also to a number of the "better" citizens of the *Posad*, to whom, on special occasions, permission was granted to distill certain additional quantities of liquor, ostensibly to be declared and delivered to the government storehouse. Often these rights were abused, and liquor thus distilled would turn up for sale in public inns and pothouses. Moreover, the latter were always able to obtain large quantities of liquor from the government storehouses for resale to the thirsty. This became a thriving and highly profitable business in spite of the government's stern measures to suppress it. The campaign against illegal selling of liquor was all the more difficult and even dangerous because the tavern keepers could buy protection from highly placed persons within the administration.

A prominent feature of the Moscow daily scene was the multitude of beggars. There were efforts on the part of the city administration to assist unfortunates by maintaining poorhouses and foundling homes. The Council of a Hundred Chapters (*Stoglav Sobor*), held in Moscow in 1551, discussed the matter of charity at length and especially stressed the need of poorhouses, but none of these efforts or recommendations ever achieved any noticeable success because they were contrary to the peculiar Russian concept of charity. For the Russian of those days, charity was not a means of fighting social ills, but rather a pious activity necessary for the salvation of one's soul. His motives in giving alms to the poor were primarily religious, largely with an eye to his own future reward. This attitude determined the character of Muscovite social service. Charity was considered to be the personal affair of a pious man, and the best possible form it could take was the giving of alms. For the Muscovite, the beggar, as an element in the exercise of piety, was no less important than the house icon. This is the reason for the extraordinary development of begging supported by the widely practiced giving of alms in old Moscow.

According to Yakov Reutenfels, Rome's ambassador to Moscow from 1670 to 1673, one could often see large crowds of beggars at the entrances to houses of the rich, waiting for food or other alms. Paul of Aleppo says that such opportunities for charity were regularly distributed among the boyar households, each one of which supported a number of beggars. Groups of beggars, usually a dozen or more, were attached to the various cathedrals and monasteries. A multitude of beggars received food from the kitchens of the tsar and the patriarch, who thus set an example for the whole of Moscow society. It was the custom of the patriarch on his public appearances to hand out alms to any beggar he happened to encounter. The usual dole was one *grivna* (onetenth of a ruble). Tsar Aleksei Mikhailovich constantly maintained in his palace several poor old men who were considered regular members of the palace staff, holding the rank of "supreme supplicants" (*verkhovyie bogomol'tsy*).

Public torture of felons was a common sight on the streets of Moscow. Often one could see an executioner leading a half-naked, blood-covered man through the streets and squares, flogging him with a knout and making loud announcement of his crime. Similar scenes could be observed near all the law enforcement offices in the Kremlin.

Thieves were punished by having their heels broken: after being allowed to rest two or three days, they were then forced to walk long distances. Serious crimes were punished by death. Victims were hanged, broken on the wheel, impaled, beaten to death, buried alive, or burned in iron cages. Women found guilty of murdering their husbands were put into specially prepared holes in the ground, earth was tightly packed up to their necks, and they were left to die. Counterfeiters were stretched on the ground and molten lead was poured down their throats. Those guilty of sacrilege were torn to pieces by iron hooks.

Capital punishment was carried out in public as were other forms of punishment. In the spirit of the age, executions were performed with great solemnity in a manner calculated to put fear into the hearts of all potential evil doers.

These executions usually took place in the large city squares—the Red and the Boloto. During the reign of Ivan the Terrible, mass executions took place even inside the Kremlin. In 1574, he put to death, in the Kremlin Cathedral Square, the abbot of the Chudov Monastery, the archpriest, and many boyars. But, generally speaking, the Kremlin was not considered the proper place for executions. It was mostly Red Square that witnessed all kinds of gruesome executions up to the end of the seventeenth century. It was there that the mass slaughter of the boyars and their retainers was carried out during the reign of the Terrible, and it was there, more than a century later, during the reign of Peter the Great, that the famous mass execution of the mutinous *streltsy* took place. V. V. Nechaev furnishes some supplementary details: "Two hundred and one *streltsy*, comprising the first section of the condemned, were executed in the presence of the Tsar on September 30, 1698. He, personally, cut off five heads. On October 11th, 144 more were executed; on the 12th—205; on the 13th—141; on the 17th—109; on the 18th—65; on the 19th—106; and on the 21st—2. Some executions were carried out in various parts of the city. One hundred and ninety-five *streltsy* were hanged from thirty-five gallows placed in front of the Novodevichei Convent, under the windows of the cell occupied by the Tsar's half sister, Princess Sophia, who was implicated in the mutiny. A number of the ringleaders among the mutineers were broken on the wheel in the Red Square and were left there to die in agony. The corpses remained lying on the square for five months; they were taken away for burial in March, 1699. Executions were started again in February, 1699, and more than 400 heads were cut off. It is said that Peter himself beheaded 84 *streltsy*."

Such were the scenes that might be witnessed on the streets of old Moscow. There were others, also, no less characteristic of Moscow life, associated only with places where business and official activities were concentrated—the Kremlin and the main Moscow market place—Red Square, with its commercial rows.

Animated activities could be observed on Ivanovskaya Square (an area to the east of the Ivan Bell Tower in the Kremlin). In the seventeenth century, a number of various law enforcement offices, courthouses, and central government administration buildings were located on this square. Office activities would begin around 7:30 A.M., and the square would start to fill up at dawn with crowds going to various offices on business. Here persons guilty of tax evasion or non-payment of debts would be lined up in rows, and bailiffs, armed with long wooden rods (*batogi*), would walk along the rows and administer punishment by beating the culprits' feet. This was the method commonly used in Muscovite Russia for collecting debts and delinquent taxes. The guilty individuals would be brought from prison or would report in person—if they were out on bail—for merciless beatings day after day until the debts were paid. The moans and howls of the victims of Muscovite justice would drown out the hubbub and bustle of the crowded square. In harmony with this motley Asiatic scene were the public scribes, clerks, and notaries presiding in their robes of office in special stalls. These functionaries had the exclusive right of executing legal documents. Owing to a long-established custom, they were allowed to exact large fees for their work, and the business was highly profitable. Cancellation of their licenses, which meant exile from the Square, was considered by them the worst possible punishment.

Ivanovskaya Square also served as a place for official government announcements. Here—as on Red Square—government criers would announce all new edicts, report news of public interest, and sometimes advertise activities planned by private individuals. V. V. Nechaev cites such a case in connection with the first aviation experiment in Russia. On this Square, in April, 1695, a *muzhik*, whose name remains unknown, began to shout for help. Taken into custody, he declared that he wanted to get the attention of the authorities to help him construct wings that would enable him to fly like a crane. The tsar, Peter the Great, on being told about it, became greatly interested and ordered that the *muzhik* should be given money for the construction of mica wings. The first experiment took place in front of the guardhouse in the presence of the military governor, Prince Troekurov, and a throng of the curious. The *muzhik* crossed himself and began to inflate the bellows of his flying machine, but failed to get off the ground. He apologized, declaring that the wings were too heavy. He was again given money to construct lighter wings, this time of leather, but the second experiment was not successful either. Troekurov stopped all further experiments, sentenced the would-be aviator to be flogged, and ordered him to return the money spent on the venture to the government.

Red Square was the center of political and social life of medieval Moscow in much the same way that the Roman Forum served ancient Rome. Here is the *Lobnoe Mesto* (Place of the Brow)—a tribune somewhat like the Roman Rostrum or the Novgorod *Veche Stepen'* (Assembly Platform)—called by some of the medieval Russian chroniclers the "umbilicus of the world." From this low, flat-topped structure the tsars delivered their speeches and the patriarchs of the church blessed the people. Tradition has it that in 1547, on this very platform, Ivan the Terrible bewailed his misrule, confessed the sins of his youth, and promised amendment. With Red Square are associated many events in Russian history. In the fourteenth century it was often the scene of bloody battles with the Tatars. In the seventeenth century it witnessed uprisings and the wholesale executions of 1698. It was also the central market place not only of Moscow but of the whole country, since the principal trade routes converged here.

Near the Spas Gates was the Krestets, where unemployed priests offered their services to merchants and boyars who had private chapels, ready to say Mass and to perform whatever rites were demanded of them for a small monetary consideration. Near by, on both sides of the former Spas Bridge, which crossed the Alevisian Moat, were the many stores and booths that sold manuscripts (later, printed books), penny prints (*lubki*), and works of local and foreign art. In Red Square scribes peddled their wares—pious religious texts, historical compilations, lives of the saints, tales of miracle workers, and—stealthily—also stories and verses of a secular nature.

The police department had its offices behind a high fence on the site of the present Historical Museum. Musketeers on duty would bring here all thieves and violators of public order.

An open, noisy, brawling market spread out in front of St. Basil's Church. Merchants crying aloud urged prospective customers to inspect their wares. Vendors circulating among the motley crowd offered *pirogi* (meatpies), *sheeten'* (hot mead), and kvas (a drink of fermented rye bread). Blind beggars sang at crossings and comedians and acrobats performed tricks and put trained bears through their paces to the great delight of the gaping throngs.

The beggars, the rouged wenches offering their charms, the peddlers, the public executions, the religious services and processions—all greatly contributed to the local color. Added to the above were the numerous pubs and taverns, the most famous of which was known as "Beneath the Cannon" (*Pod Pushkoi*). Foreign visitors were always amazed at the sight of stark-naked people who had left their last stitch of clothing at the tavern.

All day peddling and lively pushcart selling were carried on throughout the entire length of the Square. Tailors, shoemakers, and street jewelers worked at their trade under the open sky, right in the midst of the crowds, thus accentuating the oriental character of the market place. Near the *Lobnoe Mesto* women sold cloth and rings set with turquoise; in addition to their merchandise, these same women, according to Olearius, offered their customers "something else." The market extended beyond the limits of Red Square, descending the slope of the hill down to the river, to the live-fish tanks and Moskvoretsk Bridge, where there were many small booths and vegetable stands; close by, women were washing clothes in the river. Business was also conducted on the Kremlin moat bridges near the Saviour's and St. Nicholas' gates.

The greatest gatherings on Red Square usually took place on market days, on Wednesdays and Fridays, when many peasants from neighboring villages came to the city. However, even on other days, the Square attracted not only swarms of sellers and buyers, but also vast numbers of idlers and unemployed, for whom the market place was a kind of democratic club.

Rows of stalls ran in Kitai-Gorod on the old market site just east of the Kremlin walls on the bank of the Moskva River. The more important stores and commercial establishments were concentrated in rows adjoining Red Square. These were subject to tax, and since they were a source of considerable income to the government, the latter found it profitable to assign definite permanent locations for them and to provide protection from thieves and fire hazards. No living quarters within these stores were permitted, and at night special guards were stationed on the roofs in constant lookout for fires and thieves. The guards were assisted by vicious dogs chained to long cables strung along the walls.

Foreign visitors to the seventeenth-century Moscow market were greatly impressed by the system of grouping the stalls and by the ease with which one could find sought-after items, since each row or group of rows handled only specific kinds of goods. There was pleasurable excitement in the array of goods in the open market: velvets and brocades, Perisan fabrics, Arabian silver, Frankish swords, copper and damascened steel, tooled leather, and colorful pottery, to say nothing of fruits and vegetables arranged in large baskets and trays under the open sky. Western Europeans seem to have been particularly taken with the Iconographers' Row, the Fishmongers' Row and the so-called "Lousy" Market (somewhat of the nature of the Paris "Flea" Market)—all of them distinguished for their unique sights, smells, and local color. There was the unmistakable odor of spoiled fish hanging over the entire area of the Fishmongers' Row, and the European visitor was always baffled by the strange and peculiar taste shown by the Russian in eating such fish. The "Lousy" Market, according to Reutenfels, was so called because it sold all kinds of old stuff: rags, old clothes, junk, and ramshackle furniture. This market was also the place occupied by barbers who worked in low, bark-covered booths or, weather permitting, under the open sky. Here the ground was thickly strewn with hair—accumulated through the decades—forming what looked like a solid felt cover. The smell and sight of these barbers and their barbering techniques turned many a Western visitor's stomach.

The people generally dined around noon and then would rest, in accordance with national custom. Street traffic and commercial activities would come to a standstill. Shopkeepers and their assistants would stretch out and go to sleep right in front of their booths. At dusk the shops would be closed behind heavy shutters, and at night silence, almost of the grave, would descend upon the streets which a few hours earlier were swarming with humanity. The gates to the entrances and exits of the main streets would be locked, and circulation after nightfall would become difficult if not hazardous. As was the case in all cities in medieval Europe, there were frequent robberies at night. There were no street lights, and nobody stirred outdoors unless accompanied by friends or slaves with lanterns or torches. There was the peril of being brained and robbed, or of being drenched with buckets of filthy slops flung recklesly from upper windows into the streets.

Herberstein relates that in his day the Moscow thoroughfares were blocked at night by logs laid across the street and that anybody caught by the night watchmen after a certain hour would be beaten or put in prison.

Frequent fires contributed to the disruption of normal life. In the sixteenth and seventeenth centuries, a succession of terrific conflagrations devastated Moscow. No sooner had the traces of the horrible fire of 1571 (experienced by Moscow during the invasion of the Crimean horde) been erased than the city was again set on fire, in 1611, by incendiaries and reduced to ashes. The great fire of 1626—breaking out in Kitai-Gorod—spread to the commercial rows, to the Church of Basil the Blessed, and then to the Kremlin, where it destroyed the churches of the Chudov and Voznesensky monasteries, several buildings in the tsar's and patriarch's courts, and many government offices with all their vital documents. Fires again broke out in 1629, 1633, and 1634, laying waste many parts of the city. According to Olearius, there was hardly a week without a fire consuming several houses at a time ,and quite often, when the wind was strong, whole streets would go up in flames.

Various measures were applied to combat these tragic occurrences. As a preventive, the use of heating stoves in homes and public baths during the summer months was forbidden. The law was enforced by specially appointed agents, whose duty it was to inspect every house and seal up all heating stoves for the summer. A fire department was maintained, and the firemen got their wages, up to 1629, from the city. After that, their maintenance was taken over by the state, which increased the number of firemen from the previous one hundred men to two hundred. The fire-fighting equipment (pipes, barrels, buckets, and fire shields) were provided by the state treasury. For transportation—day or night—the fire department had at its disposal twenty vehicles whose drivers were recruited from the city cabmen's guild and whose duty it was to queue up at the fire department yard and await their turn. The breaking out of a fire would be announced by the nearest church bell tower; the watchmen, stationed on the Kremlin walls and towers, would immediately respond by tolling the bells of the particular tower facing the part of the city where the fire was raging. The standard method of fighting a fire was to localize it, that is, to demolish the buildings in the path of the fire and remove all combustible material, thus preventing its spread.

Robbery and murder were no less chronic than fires. At night the city would be taken over by holdup men and thieves, and hardly a night would pass without several murders. Every morning the police would pick up the dead lying in the streets, bring all the unidentified bodies to the City Yard, and leave them there for identification by relatives or friends. Unidentified bodies would be taken to the poorhouse, where they were kept, along with the bodies of executed criminals, those who died in prison, and those dead of excessive drinking, until Trinity Week, when they were buried in a common grave. The citizens of Moscow were so terrorized by nightly robberies that nobody dared to respond to cries for help; citizens were even afraid to approach the windows to see what was going on. Burglary was just as frequent as street robbery.

It is interesting to note, Nechaev points out, that the main contingent of robbers and burglars was supplied by the boyars' households. It was customary for the latter to have tens and hundreds of retainers and servants, but it was not customary to provide food or decent shelter. They lived on the boyars' premises in miserable huts—no better than pigstys—half-starved on a diet of garbage. No wonder these desperate menials would try to obtain food and clothing by burglary and robbery.

The police were not strong enough numerically to cope with the crime problem. Their helplessness would become especially apparent during the general Shrovetide revelries, when the guards on watch would themselves get drunk and the incidence of street murders would greatly increase. The boyars hired special guards to stand night watch over their courts and hourly announce their presence by striking a wooden board with a stick. Olearius ventures the opinion that these guards often connived with the thieves and helped them get inside the boyars' courts, loot their homes, and then disappear.

Life in the Moscow of those days was indeed grim and insecure. Most of it was filled with anxiety and incessant threats: today you were burned out of your home; tomorrow the invading enemy were at the gates of your city; the next day, the plague or the famine; the night before, there was a fiery apparition in the sky, a portent of great troubles to come. And over this unhappy life the stern spirit of the church, damning, threatening with everlasting punishment. But whatever its troubles, life in old Moscow was not dull and spiritless. The air was always filled with the pent-up energy, the hum and buzz of the seething, turbulent, long-suffering masses, and one never knew when it might become dangerously violent and murderous. We have only to recall the frequent uprisings that took place in Moscow during the sixteenth and seventeenth centuries.

The streets were crowded and exciting. Carts, produce wagons, and mounted boyars made their way through a walking populace of tradespeople, artisans and laborers, serfs and peasants from the countryside, priests, beggars, thieves, harlots, and respectable housewives.

A bewildering variety of buildings filled the city. There were hundreds of churches and chapels, poorhouses and foundling homes, masonry palaces of the great nobles, homes of well-to-do merchants, hovels of the working people, innumerable taverns and inns, brothels and baths, markets, spice shops, and bakeries scattered throughout the city.

During the day, the tempo of street life was brisk. The liveliest activities occurred where people congregated the most—the Kremlin, Red Square, and the adjoining commercial rows. But even in the other parts of the city, traffic was heavy—this is attested to by the large number of Moscow cabmen. According to Reutenfels, a number of cabs or sleighs were stationed at each street crossing and at every city gate. The cab drivers were efficient, and transportation was fast and inexpensive.

Here and there in the main streets one would see noble ladies riding in gaily decorated vehicles: closed horse-drawn carriages in the summer or sleighs covered with red taffeta in the winter. Olearius describes these feminine outings as having all the attributes of a theatrical spectacle: the lady would be sitting in the sleigh "in all the splendor of a goddess," a slave girl at her feet, and thirty to forty servants running at the sides. Her "serene highness" would be leaning back on her cushions with a studied attitude of indifference and boredom, letting the whole street take in the splendor of her furs and richly embroidered clothes, the pearls and gems which embellished her *kokoshnik* (headdress). The horses were caparisoned with foxtails, which, by the way, were also used by noblemen when riding out on gala occasions. Officials and well-to-do people rode horseback; young dandies could be seen on their horses with richly ornamented bridles and gold-embroidered saddle cloths.

The toiling mass of the people had its own spectacles and amusements: In the streets there were trained animals, jugglers, acrobats, and musicians. The whole city would turn out to watch the spectacular parades and processions on occasions of great religious festivals and national holidays, when the patriarch and the tsar would pass through the Kremlin *Spas* (Saviour's) Gates on the way to Red Square.

The streets would take on a holiday look during the rare occasions when the tsar would show himself to his people. The unhappy memories of Ivan the Terrible's appearances— when the tsar's black-robed special guards (*oprichniki*) used to terrorize the citizenry—had all but faded. The seventeenth-century Romanovs cultivated an aura of divine superiority: they lived a secluded life in their palaces and were inaccessible to the people. Whenever they did make an appearance, the very way it was staged only accentuated their separateness. The tsar's cortege would follow a predetermined route; the chosen streets would be swept clean and guards stationed at strategic points. The cortege would be headed by a company of *streltsy* armed with long rods followed by a second company of *streltsy*. The tsar's carriage would be surrounded by a crowd of boyars and courtiers. Any people found in the way of the cortege would be beaten and dispersed; a few brave souls would hug the walls, stand reverently, or prostrate themselves at the approach of the tsar's carriage.

Moscow streets would also take on a holiday look on the special days when foreign ambassadors would be received in solemn audience by the tsar. The government would line the route appointed for the ambassadors' passage with huge throngs of servitors, functionaries, and townspeople. Stores would close, and all market places would be cleared of peddlers and buyers. All this was done for the purpose of heightening the prestige of the tsar in the eyes of the foreigners and the native population, to impress the foreigners with the size of the capital's population, and to demonstrate to the people the might of the tsar to whom these resplendent foreign ambassadors were to pay their respects.

The church appealed to the theatrical sense of the masses by the magnificence of its ceremonies. The most solemn religious processions took place on the sixth of January, Epiphany Day, and on Palm Sunday—both handsomely and dramatically staged.

On the sixth of January, the Jordan Ceremony, or the Blessing of the Waters, would be performed at the Moskva River near the Tainitskaya Tower. Detachments of *streltsy* would be lined up inside the Kremlin and along the bank of the river. The tsar himself in full regalia would head the procession, followed by court officials, military officers of the highest rank, and prominent merchants, all in their parade uniforms. The banks of the river, the roofs of neighboring houses, and the Kremlin walls would be covered by throngs of spectators.

The most spectacular of these pageants was the Palm Sunday Procession: a vast slow-moving religious drama staged on Red Square against the background of the Kremlin, in which the tsar and the patriarch played the chief parts, their attendants—the boyars, the massed clergy—the minor roles. The procession depicted the entrance of Jesus into Jerusalem. Olearius, who witnessed the ceremony on April 10, 1636, described it: "The procession wending its way from the Kremlin to the Jerusalem Church [St. Basil's on the Red Square], was slowly moving along in the following manner:

"Heading the procession was a very large, wide but quite low wagon on which was mounted a tree hung with many apples, figs, and raisins. In the tree were four young boys in white surplices, singing Hosanna.

"The wagon was followed by many priests in richly embroidered white vestments glittering with precious stones and pearls. They carried banners, crosses, and icons mounted on long staffs—all singing in unison. Some carried censers, swaying them toward the people lining the procession. Behind the clergy walked Moscow's most prominent merchants, followed by court officials, scribes, secretaries, and by princes and boyars waving palm branches.

"Next came the gorgeously robed Tsar, wearing his crown and attended by the ranking princes of the of the realm. The Tsar himself led the patriarch's cloth-covered horse, whose ears were artfully lengthened, simulating the ears of an ass. The Patriarch rode his 'ass' sideways. His head was covered with a white, round cap richly embellished with large pearls and surmounted by a crown. In his right hand he held a gold gem-studded cross with which he was blessing the people; the latter responding by bowing their heads very low and reverently crossing themselves. Alongside and behind the Patriarch walked the metropolitans, the bishops, and other priests carrying either sacred books or censers. There also were about fifty young men dressed mostly in red. At the approach of the Tsar, some of them would remove their coats and spread them along the path; others would unroll large pieces of varicolored cloth and cover the road to be traveled by the Tsar and the Patriarch." Olearius asserts that customarily the patriarch paid the tsar two hundred rubles for leading his simulated ass.

He further comments on the way the Russians celebrate Easter: "Easter Sunday is a day of great merriment for the Russians. First, because it is the day of Christ's Resurrection; second because it marks the end of their long fast. On this day and all through the next fourteen days, absolutely everybody—the princes of the realm, and the lowly peasants, the young and the old—provides himself with colored eggs. Everywhere on the streets there are numberless peddlers selling hard-boiled varicolored eggs.

"When they meet on the street, they greet each other with a kiss on the lips—one exclaims: 'Christ has risen,' the other answers: 'Verily He has risen.'

"And positively nobody, neither man nor woman, the greatest of magnates or the lowliest peasant would deny the other such a kiss and greeting, nor the gift of a colored egg. The Tsar himself would give such eggs to his courtiers and retainers. On Easter eve, before attending Mass, the Tsar would visit the prisons and present each prisoner with an egg and a sheepskin coat, remarking, 'Let them be joyful, since Christ who died for their sins has now verily risen.' "

Such were the official celebrations and festivities in which only the representatives of the church and state were active as performers while the common people were limited to the role of mere spectators. However, there were purely folk holidays, or feast days, when the common people would take over the streets and assume the role of organizers and actors.

Remnants of paganism and of various superstitious cults still lingered on, reflected in the manner of celebrating certain holidays. The annual pagan holidays were closely intertwined with the Christian. The celebration of the New Year bore the Russian name *Kolyada*, and coincided with Christmas. The ritual side of the celebration remained purely pagan: on Christmas Eve the people in many parts of Russia, until quite recent times, held a ritual feast symbolizing a prayer for abundance and welfare in the coming year. Christmas fortunetelling marked the period from Christmas to Epiphany.

Shrovetide, which was not recognized by the church, continued to exist on its own. The summer holiday was connected with St. John's Day. The purely Christian holiday of Easter was combined with the holiday of the Sun and Perun (the pagan god of thunder). In some parts of Russia "Holy Week" was called "Thunder Week" (the belief existed that thunder during "Holy Week" presaged a good harvest). Perun was replaced by the prophet Elijah. The holiday of Yarila, an ancient Slavonic spring holiday, also continued to live on, although the *Stoglav sobor* fought against it. Friday was also made a holiday in honor of the goddess Lada, a rite long preserved in the Ukraine, where the weekly holiday, even as late as the sixteenth century, was not Sunday but Friday.

The so-called "evil spirits," who corresponded to the pagan gods of evil that brought misfortunes upon people, were completely absorbed into the Russified Christian conceptions. Witches and sorcerers, the mediums of the evil spirits, remained in the life of the people in spite of the church's fight against them.

Although folk feast days were largely timed to coincide with church holidays, they have never lost their secular character. The outstanding feature of these holiday celebrations was wholesale drunken debauchery. Everybody, including the clergy, got drunk. Johann Korb, the secretary of the Austrian Embassy in 1698–99, asserts that women were first to start carousing. On Easter Sundays, one could see them on almost every street: "pale, half-naked, and utterly shameless." Drunken men and women were lying everywhere, some of them dead, without a stitch of clothing. A by-product of this debauchery was fire: there was hardly a holiday without fire breaking out in one or several parts of the city.

Christmas was the time of hilarious street carnivals. On Christmas Eve, and for the next twelve days, bands of men and women wearing masquerade costumes would invade the streets. Patriarch Yoachim (in his edict of 1684) describes the Christmastide merrymakers as people who have lost all human semblance: "Old and young put on idolatrous and satanic masks and with devilish cunning tempt orthodox Christians with dances and similar craftiness."

The church and the pious Tsar Aleksei were especially outraged with the portrayal of a very popular masquerade scene in which the leading character, called *Kobylka* (little mare), was given great prominence. The Tsar in his edict of 1648 called it "satanic." The masqueraders danced and sang bawdy songs interspersed with the kind of ribald folk humor which the church equated with obscenity.

An important role in the Christmastide revelries was played by the "Chaldeans"—the actors in the dramatized version of the story of the three Hebrew youths, Shadrach, Meshach, and Abednego, cast into the fiery furnace. This play, which became known as the "Fiery Furnace," was usually performed during the church service on the Saturday before Christmas. Giles Fletcher (*The Russe Commonwealth* [London, 1591]) described it as: "A pageant they have the weeke before the Nativitie of Christ; when every bishop in his Cathedral Church setteth forth the show of three children in the oven. When an Angell is made to come flying from the roofs of the church with great admiration of the lookers-on, and many terrible flashes of fire are made with Drosen and gunpowder by the Chaldeans."

According to the Russian art historian Nikodim Kondakov, the name "Chaldeans" was attached at the beginning of the seventeenth century to bands of jesters or mummers, who used to wander through the streets of Moscow at Christmastime putting on shows for purposes of advertising their forthcoming miracle play. They would often get out of hand and run though the streets in bands with burning pine torches, indulging in all sorts of pranks and rough horseplay at the cost of the populace, setting fire to the beards of passing pedestrians and scaring the life out of the simple-minded peasants by their outlandish appearance and nasty tricks. The Chaldeans wore tall, painted wooden hats suggesting that they were the Babylonian slaves of King Nebuchadnezzar, getting ready to make the furnace "exceedingly hot" for the three Hebrew youths.

These masked jesters were considered by the church as unclean, contaminated by evil spirits, and on Baptism Day they would be forced to go through the ceremony of purification by immersion in the river ice holes. Patriarch Nikon discontinued the performance of the "Fiery Furnace" play and forbade the Chaldeans to appear on the streets.

In the spring, during Trinity Week, special holidays would be celebrated, which were essentially pagan. *Semik*, the Thursday preceding Trinity Day, was dedicated to the *Rusalki* (mermaids, water-nymphs), and these festivities became known as *rusalii*. Trinity Saturday was Cemetery Day. It would begin with church services and visits to the graves and then wind up at the cemetery with a feast of *bliny* (pancakes) followed by songs and dances.

Another form of mass amusement were the exhibition fist fights arranged for the young people, such as those described by Herberstein: "The youths and boys usually have a large open space in the city, where they assemble on holidays and can be seen and heard by the people. They assemble at a given signal, which is a certain sort of whistle, after which they run off and fight among themselves. First they strike and punch one another with their fists; but soon with their knees and feet too, striking at random, as hard as they can, in the throat, the chest, the belly, and the genitals or wherever else they can. In the struggle for victory one will fling another down in such a way that they are often carried off half-dead. The one who is most often victor, remains last on the spot, and most bravely bears blows, carries off the glory. They have this sort of competition so that the boys may get used to giving blows and receiving punches." These fist fights, although frowned upon by the church and state, were very popular, since they satisfied the people's craving for spectacle and amusement; they took root and, in time, developed into a national sport practiced until recent times.

A prominent role in all these festivities and revelries was played by the *Skomorokhi*—the wandering minstrels, buffoons, and primitive professional entertainers of medieval Russia—the precursors of the brilliant actors and producers of the Russian nineteenth-century theater. Their origin is obscure: they may have drifted into Moscow from Poland and Lithuania as wandering actors, or they may have come, in earlier times, to Kiev from the court of Byzantium, famous for its mimes and professional entertainers. At the courts of the Kiev princes, we find them as singers and tellers of tales. Later the great boyars as well as the tsar kept them as clowns whose business it was to entertain by composing running commentaries on people and events.

The *Skomorokhi* usually took an active part in all public festivals and ceremonies. They would gather the celebrants around themselves and perform all kinds of amusing tricks; they sang and danced, initiated and directed mass singing and dancing, and improvised humorous and racy dialogues on social and political themes. These lusty improvisations became, in time, fixed by oral tradition and later developed into boisterous and bawdy street farces.

One of the more spectacular ritual ceremonies in which the *Skomorokhi* usually took an active part was the marriage ceremony. Different members of the family had parts set for them by tradition, the most dramatic role being given to the bride. The general theme of the drama is the siege of the bride, who calls on her brothers to defend her and her mother to pity her. This elaborate performance varied in detail in different districts, but in all versions the "friends" and matchmakers played the comic roles.

The wandering puppet theater of the seventeenth century was basically the same as that of more recent times. It was of course more primitive in its staging techniques: The *Skomorokh* comedian used a large piece of cloth or a bed cover, the lower part of which was fastened to his body and folded in such a way that the upper part could be raised above his head, thus forming a portable stage—leaving him free to walk along the streets, stop at any point, and manipulate his puppets. The repertoire of this theater and its principal characters seems to have undergone very little change. In the illustrations of the puppet plays left to us by Olearius we find among the principal characters of the dramatis personae the traditional Petrushka, the Gypsy, and Petrushka's bride Variushka. We see Petrushka examining the horse that the Gypsy is trying to sell him—a scene which survives to this day. There was also the cynical and frankly lascivious scene, the so-called "Petrushka's Wedding," played by Petrushka and Variushka. Olearius commented that these puppeteers "show their puppets, representing their brutalities and sodomies, make sport to the children, who are thereby induced to quit all sentiments of shame and honesty."

The ascetic and militant church, hostile to secular society and its way of life, recognized in all these worldly folk activities the survivals of paganism. From its point of view, all manifestations of the folk creative genius were the invention of the devil, incompatible with the spirit of a Christian society. The Patriarch Yoasaf (1634–42) was especially horrified by the antics of the *Skomorokhi*, their suggestive dancing, reciting, and singing. He ordered all musical instruments to be taken away from the wandering players and destroyed. Then he issued a decree forbidding all instrumental music and ordered all musical instruments found in private homes to be burned. The final blow to the activities of the *Skomorokhi* was administered during the reign of the pious and "most quiet" Tsar Aleksei Mikhailovich when a systematic drive was launched to suppress all folk merrymaking, without exception. An edict was issued (in 1648) denying people the right "to dance, to play games or watch them; at wedding feasts either to sing or play on instruments; or to give over one's soul to perdition in such pernicious and lawless practices as word-play, farces or magic. To wear masks or *skomorokhi* clothes, to be *skomorokhi* or to play on *gusli*, *bubni*, *gudki* [Russian musical instruments]. Offenders for the first and second offense to be beaten with rods, for the third and fourth to be banished to the border towns." (P. I. Ivanov)

These repressive measures were strictly applied and evidently succeeded, up to a degree, in accomplishing their purpose. They were especially successful in the fight against the activities of the *Skomorokhi*, resulting in their disappearance by the beginning of the eighteenth century. Life in Moscow thus acquired a veneer of propriety, but lost some of the wild vitality and spontaneity characteristic of its medieval period.

CHAPTER FOUR

MOSCOW ARCHITECTURE

Early Structures

THE vast forests of the Northeast region profoundly influenced the development of Muscovite architecture. For generations the entire utilitarian and artistic environment of the Russian peasant was fashioned of wood, and it was this constant close contact with the forests that contributed so much to the arts of woodcraft and the great skill of the Russian carpenter. Building in wood acquired a very special place in the history of Russian architecture; and its distinctive and most typical forms were closely bound up, in their origin, with the virtues and limitations of wood. Because of the advantages in comfort and warmth that wooden structures offered in a cold climate, the huts and hovels of the lowly and most of the old Moscow palaces and mansions of the rich and mighty were built of wood.

The structural development of Russian wood architecture is a fascinating story of the mutations and combinations of the various forms of blockwork: the rectangle and the polygon; types of roof (shed, wedge, ogee barrel vault, and tent); and storied belfries, pinnacles, and cupolas. In the period of the rise of Moscow the influence of these forms was so decisive that the history of Moscow architecture is, to a great degree, that of translating and adapting wooden architectural forms to masonry structures.

The basic form in Russian wooden construction is the blockwork rectangular frame formed by round logs laid horizontally in ranges and interlocking at the corners. The rectangular frame was the unit of wood construction forming the principal element of the Russian workingman's or peasant's cottage, the *izba*. It was covered by a gabled roof, and in olden times had no ceiling. This simple structure had an importance in the development of Russian wooden architecture greater than some of the more pretentious edifices. The *izba* is essentially a heated chamber, in its earliest and simplest forms lacking a chimney, the windows serving as an outlet for smoke. For protection against cold and dampness, door and window openings were reduced to a minimum. Living quarters of the well-to-do were on the second floor; the ground floor was usually reserved for servants and storage. Large houses consisting of several units and two or three floors were called *khoromy* (mansions, manors) or *dvortsy* (palaces).

The simplest form of roof was the gable, but the Russian craftsman, with his flair for the picturesque, was quick to see possibilities for modifications and variations. A range of varying effects and expressions was developed from the sloping roof of the common hut to the wedgelike roofs, peaked gables, and ogee-shaped pyramidal and multi-domed roofs of the great churches.

The window became the focus for rich decoration that often extended several feet on each side of it, sometimes over the entire height of the building. In brick buildings the window was set into a fancifully arched frame, the whole incrusted with colored tiles. The cottage window frame was also accentuated and often was treated in a delightfully fanciful way. In this, Russian builders have persevered through the centuries with considerable success, so that the most beautiful feature of the village and town cottages are the windows framed by masses of carved and painted ornament, relieving the severity of unadorned log walls.

The stairway received much attention. In Moscow, as in other medieval Russian cities, the role of the exterior stairway was not limited to the merely practical function of getting to or from the upper floors. The stairway and its landings served as a setting for the display of hospitality, manners, and customs. On the landings the formal welcoming of guests and visitors took place, and it was there that the ceremony of bidding them good-by was performed. Thus etiquette gave importance to the arrangement, construction, and decoration of the stairway.

The basic elements of even the very sumptuous mansions were still the blockwork frames and their connecting vestibules. Most of the units were two-storied, and the appellation *khoromy* was, in a proper sense, attached only to the upper or elevated stories which contained the private apartments of the owner. As in the yard of the peasant, so in the very extensive court of the boyar, each blockwork unit was built separately and at some distance from the others, the space between the units depending on their functional relationship and the available ground. As a whole, the wooden mansion was nearly always an ensemble of units of a decorative and picturesque character, more or less flamboyant. Instead of the Western European single-unit mansion or palace, the Russian builder usually erected a group of interconnected structures, and although he evidently had little feeling for formal symmetry, he was endowed with a surpassing sense

97

of balance. Varied in size, form, and outline as his units were, they were nearly always arranged to produce a feeling of unity and balance; but at the same time the builder never suppressed his love of romantic composition, play of light and shade, and vivid colors.

Perhaps one of the best examples of ancient *khoromy* architecture is the celebrated, but now vanished, tsar's palace—"the Russian Versailles"—at Kolomenskoe near Moscow. Some idea of it can be had from the existing model made shortly before the aging and crumbling structure was taken down in 1768 by order of Catherine II. The palace, set in gardens on a high bluff overlooking the Moskva River, was in reality a small city complex consisting of 270 block-work dwelling units of various shapes and sizes. It contained all the characteristic elements of the great mansions: the vestibules with their elaborately decorated stairways, passageways, arcaded balconies, towers, and observation platforms. Here also were all the roof forms, the varied shapes of doors and windows, and the multifarious decorative entablatures developed throughout the centuries.

Much like the seventeenth-century Moscow Kremlin, the palace at Kolomenskoe was a product of national art. Its architectural forms reflect the imagery of the folk poetry and the fairy tale of the magic Fire-Bird (*Zhar-Ptitsa*) Palace glittering with gold and bright colors. The roots of this architecture can be traced to the mythical age of pagan Russia and its growth and perfection to the provinces of the Northeast.

These elaborate, ornate stairways, observation towers, communicating arcades, and galleries have influenced the design of many recent structures in masonry as well as in wood. The model of the palace served as a reference source for the nineteenth-century architects who tried to revive the architecture of Russian antiquity, and it is evident that the architects of the Historical Museum (Sherwood) and the Municipal Duma (Chichagov), in present-day Moscow, were inspired by it.

Wooden Churches

Long before Christianity became the official faith of Russia Christian churches existed, and there is very little doubt about the material of which they were constructed. It was mainly in the North and the Northeast that the forms of wood building were perfected, and, as the Russian art historians Gornostaev and Grabar remark, "these forms became the inexhaustible source from which the arts of Russia, in their anemic periods, drew new blood: their significance has not been as yet fully appreciated."

The construction methods and terminology were evolved early. The old word *khoromy* was later applied to indicate the building of a *khram* or mansion, but in this case a temple, a "House of God" is meant.

Although the church was built in the fashion of an elaborate nobleman's mansion, it was felt that it required a further distinction, which was given by the addition of cupolas and crosses to the roof. The cupola was borrowed from the masonry church, but the method of wooden roof construction consigned it to the role of a purely decorative appendage. The wooden cupola, though given the circular form of the masonry domes, was modeled along different lines. Its walls were flared outward, and its top was drawn upwards and thus molded somewhat in the shape of an onion bulb. Another feature of the masonry churches, the semicircular form of the parapets built directly over the extrados of the roof vaulting (the *zakomara*), found its equivalent expression in wooden architecture. The forms that designated and accentuated the masonry roof vaulting caught the eye of the Russian builder, ever alert for novelty of design. He became cognizant of their functional virtues as well as their decorative possibilities, and adapted them to the wooden roof. The masonry semicircular parapet was given an ogee shape. Before long the barrel vault was molded to the taste of the builder in wood. The original semicircular section became an ogee section; its outline was refashioned—the walls were pushed in at the base, flared out at the center, and drawn together and shaped into a sharp ridge line at the top. This became the favorite motif of Russian builders, who varied its profile, combined it with other motifs, and used it functionally and decoratively. The *bochka* roof was usually applied to the church sanctuary and the narthex. Occasionally it served as a base for the cupolas, and often it was used over the main landing of the stairway. The profile of the *bochka* roof—its front elevation—became known as the *kokoshnik,* a form which acquired great popularity in the decorative arts, ecclesiastical and secular. The degree can be judged by the widespread use of its form in the profiling of the upper part of the icon frames, wood and metal triptychs, baldachins, and women's hair ornaments and headdresses.

Certain general plan dispositions dictated by the special requirements of the Greek Orthodox church had to be followed, but even these were greatly modified and changed to suit native building precepts, the topography, and landscape. Thus a folkish understanding of what a "House of God" should look like and how it should be built was developed. These factors irresistibly directing the development of wooden church architecture away from alien traditions gradually brought about liberation from Byzantium and influenced the modification of the once borrowed forms.

The commonest type of chapel is a blockwork rectangular structure similar to the village peasant hut—the *izba* with a simple porch in front and a cross on the roof. Churches of the rectangular tradition were evolved by the juxtaposition in a straight line of several units. The basic framework is a square or oblong box, and the most usual form of church has three units, of which the central one—the largest and tallest—is the nave; the other two, added to the east and west ends, are respectively the sanctuary and a kind of vestibule or porch (*trapeznaya* or *pritvor*) corresponding to the narthex of Byzantine and Romanesque churches. In this type the central compartment was usually given a wedge-shaped roof, crowned by a small bulbous dome covered with shingles.

No doubt the first Christian churches and chapels in Russia were of the primitive rectangular type. But at some remote period, one cannot state just when or how, a new form came into being, the octagon. Such a church, even if it lacked the crowning cross, would attract attention by its unusual form. Here the rows or logs are arranged to form a circle, or rather its nearest equivalent, an octagon, and the entire blockwork unit is covered over by a roofing system that had never been applied to an *izba*—a roof having eight slopes, something akin to a tent.

The tent type of church, while keeping the three traditional parts—the sanctuary, nave, and narthex—differed from the *izba* type in that its central element forms an octagon; being much taller, it was also distinguished by a quality of soaring verticality. The practical advantage of the octagonal form is, of course, the larger floor space gained by timbers of the same length as those used to frame the rectangle. Moreover, it is stiffer structurally, offers greater resistance to wind stresses, and therefore can be carried to a considerable height. The same is true of the tent-shaped roof, which can withstand wind velocities much greater than can the large areas of the steep gable roofs. But the most important advantage of the tented churches was inherent in the focusing or centering quality of the octagonal nucleus to whose principal axes could be added various projections giving the structure a cross-shaped form. Furthermore, it could be easily surrounded with many secondary elements—chapels, porches, galleries, and stairways. The subsidiary ridged *bochka*-shaped roofs and decorative *kokoshniki* over the secondary elements gave the ensemble an unusually picturesque and expressive silhouette.

As in churches of the rectangular plan, the floor is generally at some height above the ground. For an approach to the church, a double stairway with balustrade and roof was almost always added to the western end and sometimes made the object of elaborate ornamentation, while the rest of the church remained plain. Often a covered gallery or balcony, a few feet above ground, runs around the western part of the church.

This type of church was the most striking creation of the Russians in the field of architecture. It is remarkable how rational, how carefully thought out is this deeply national form. It was the favorite design probably because it satisfied a basic craving for verticality and vigorous silhouette. The tent-type church, though simple in its primitive form, led to greater things. Most of the novel stone forms of sixteenth-century ecclesiastical architecture seem to have been influenced by the tented wooden churches of northeastern Russia. It is this particular form that the church authorities objected to so strenuously and tried to suppress. In the eyes of the upper ranks of the clergy, the tent roof did not express the essence of the church; it seemed to them too folkish, too playful, implying too great a self-assertion on the part of the individual builder. This attitude finally culminated in a church edict issued in the middle of the seventeenth century prohibiting the construction of tent churches.

At the turn of the fifteenth century, when Western Europe was producing the great monuments of Renaissance art, efforts were made in and around Moscow to construct large stone churches. It was the primitive art of the country as exemplified in wooden architecture that formed the basis for the Muscovite Renaissance. The creative work of the new period is best described as a gradual nationalization of the forms created in Vladimir-Suzdal, Novgorod, and Pskov.

The Structures of the Kremlin

The Muscovite period is marked by many completely new developments in architecture. It is significant that even when foreign architects were called in during the rebuilding of the Moscow Kremlin and its churches, they did not reproduce Western models but apparently worked under definite directions from their Muscovite patrons and in styles that corresponded to Russian aesthetic canons.

Two churches in the Kremlin represent the work of foreign consultants. The first is the Cathedral of the Assumption, built by Ridolfo Fioravanti of Bologna in 1475–79. Begun by Russian builders, this church collapsed during the earthquake of 1472. Fioravanti based his structure on the Assumption at Vladimir, but considerably simplified the design, since he copied only the older central part. The dimensions of the cathedral are rather small, but it is so fraught with recollections, so crowded with furnishings, frescoes, and icons, from the floor to the cupola, that its smallness of space is forgotten in the fullness of its contents. The fine situation of the cathedral, its splendid domes and internal grandeur, all excite attention. Its connection with the ecclesiastical, civil, and political history of Russia gives it more than ordinary importance.

Russian historians (Solov'ev, Zabelin) point out that neither Fioravanti nor the other foreign architects had a free hand in the design of the commissioned buildings. That the Assumption Cathedral at Vladimir was suggested to Fioravanti as a model can be explained on the ground that the design of a great cathedral, the very See of the Orthodox faith, could hardly be entrusted to a foreigner, a Roman Catholic at that. Byzantine traditions were still very strong, and the Russian clergy would not tolerate revolutionary innovations in church design. On the other hand, many wooden churches in the Moscow of that period had little in common with Byzantine forms—suggesting that there were no fixed types of church architecture.

The Moscow Assumption Cathedral resembles its Vladimir namesake but is far from being a literal copy. The two cathedrals are of the same width, but the Moscow one is much longer; the Moscow cathedral has five apses, the Vladimir three; furthermore, the latter's choir galleries are suppressed. The vaulting of the Moscow Assumption rests on six pillars, four of which—huge circular columns—support the central cupola, which rests on a flat roof and is surrounded with four smaller cupolas. This very simple disposition produces a grandiose effect, and the massive pillars give an extraordinary stability without heaviness to the body of the cathedral. The influence of the Vladimir architecture is noticeable mainly in the façade, decorated at mid-height with a band or arcatures forming small niches that the architect used very successfully as window embrasures.

The Cathedral of Archangel Michael, built in 1509 by the Milanese architect Alevisio Novy, is of still greater interest. In its ground plan and in the use of five cupolas, the church presents almost a complete repetition of the Assumption in smaller dimensions. Like Fioravanti before him, Novy was compelled to incorporate the basic features of Orthodox church planning and design into the new cathedral, but in the exterior decoration he succeeded in introducing Italian architectural forms of the fifteenth century, which were adapted and reworked by Russian artists of later generations. The cathedral rests on a stone base; the lower story is embellished with pilasters and arcatures containing small windows; the upper is divided into rectangles crowned with elaborate cornices. Novy treated the *zakomary* as purely decorative features by converting them into scallop-shell niches. The result was a structure endowed with a beauty radically different from that of the preceding Moscow churches. If the Assumption Cathedral can be considered the epitome of the past and the embodiment of the traditional Moscow and Vladimir forms, the Archangel Michael was the first step toward a new art—the adaptation of the contribution that Italian art made to Moscow architecture.

The Cathdral of the Annunciation differs in certain details from the other two cathedrals of the Kremlin. The central cubical element, surmounted by five cupolas resembles the forms of the Vladimir Assumption Cathedral. In the Cathedral of the Annunciation, however, the Pskov architects introduced a motif destined to play an important role in the development of Moscow architecture of the sixteenth century and to become a theme for endless variations in the field of the decorative arts—the *kokoshnik*. The form, borrowed from the ogee-shaped roof, indicated a tendency to replace the forms of the Byzantine arch by more elongated silhouettes. The elements of the superstructure are supported with corbeled arches arranged in tiers and receding in steps. The cupola drums consequently seem to grow out of these elements, and the semicircular *zakomary* of the Vladimir and Moscow Assumption cathedrals acquire the characteristic shape of the ogee arch.

In 1547 the Cathedral of the Annunciation was damaged by a fire. While it was being repaired, open porches were added to three of its sides, the first use of a feature that became popular in the Moscow churches of the second half of the seventeenth century. At the time of the construction of the porches an anonymous Italian built the deep-shadowed portals with their engaged columns, pilasters, and archivolts, and decorated them with the richly carved, dark blue and gold ornament that winds and twists around the arches, columns, and door architraves. The Russians restudied and reworked this ornamentation, transforming it into something more suited to their taste and introducing their own ornamental elements—the *busy* (a type of beading) and the *perekhvaty* (a type of belt or band ornament).

The Tower of Ivan Veliky (Ivan the Great) stands on the brow of the hill to the east of and nearly equidistant from the Cathedrals of the Assumption and the Archangel Michael. Situated almost exactly in the center of the Kremlin and rising above the gleaming cupolas, multi-colored spires, and shining crosses of the surrounding cathedrals and palaces, this tower commands the entire scene and consolidates the various groups into one architectural composition. The Ivan

Tower, including the cross, is 270 feet high; it rests on a stone foundation, the bottom of which is said to extend down to the level of the Moskva River. The base is of white stone, and the walls are of brick reinforced with iron bars. The lower stories are octagonal in plan, receding progressively in size and height and leading up to a cylindrical drum crowned by a cupola and terminated by a large cross.

The entire composition of the tower is based on the principle of lightening the successive architectural masses as they rise, progressing from the large, heavy, simple elements at the bottom to the smaller, lighter, more complicated at the top—carrying them, as it were, through the cross into space. The effectiveness of this design is largely the result of the subtle transition from the dominant horizontality below to the verticality and broken lines of the architectural elements above. The imposing structure is a definite expression of an age, of a political and social era, reflecting the tastes, material aspirations, and political ambitions of Tsar Boris Godunov, who dreamed of perpetuating his dynasty. It is as though Godunov felt that by erecting it he had created a symbol of grandeur, a monument dominating everything created before him by the House of Rurik.

The Ivan Tower owes much of its imposing effect to its elevation and singularly conspicuous site. The placing of the huge tower in this spot created a salient vertical axis, commanding the neighboring cathedrals and all the other towers of the Kremlin. This axis of the Kremlin became at the same time the axis of all Moscow.

The Ivan Tower is the dominant element in a group of three contiguous buildings erected at different dates but forming one unit. The central and oldest part of this group is the Bono Tower, begun in 1532 and finished in 1543, antedating the Tower of Ivan by some sixty years. The Bono Tower is a four-story structure from which rises a two-story belfry that houses the principal bell of Moscow. This belfry is surmounted by a cylindrical tower of considerable height crowned by a golden cupola terminating in a cross. The architect used ancient Russian belfries as models but developed a complex architectural composition.

The second building of this group, the Tower of Patriarch Philaret, was built in 1624 during the reign of Philaret's son, Mikhail Feodorovich, the first Romanov. The main tower is four stories high; a fifth story of arches is topped by a central tent-shaped spire surrounded by Gothic turrets. This tower formerly housed the great Patriarchal Sacristy, with its priceless collection of ancient ecclesiastical art.

The first civil masonry structures were erected by Ivan III, not for residential purposes, but for formal, official needs. In 1487, Ivan III commissioned the Italian architect Marco Ruffo to build the Palace of the Facets (*Granovitaya Palata*), which was to serve him and many of his successors as a formal location for throne and audience chamber. This gray stone building, the oldest civil structure in Moscow, stands on the west side of Cathedral Square, adjoining the huge cream-colored mass of the nineteenth-century Grand Palace. Its construction was begun by Marco Ruffo but was finished by his compatriot Pietro Solario. The diamond rustications of the original façade recall the wall treatment of the Castello in Ferrara and the Pitti Palace in Florence. The Granovitaya, together with the Holy Vestibule to the west of it, is all that remains of the old palace of Ivan III. The Holy Vestibule was renovated during the construction of the Grand Kremlin Palace in 1847.

The palace contains a large, square, vaulted chamber,

about seventy-seven by seventy feet, whose size and effect of spaciousness are greatly accentuated by the single central massive pier, which made possible the use of four cross vaults to span the entire room. The chamber was admirably adapted for the great formal receptions of foreign ambassadors, the installations of the metropolitans and patriarchs, and the openings of the national assemblies. In the west wall of the chamber, close to the ceiling, is a curtained opening through which the distaff members of the royal family could observe the ceremonies from an upper-level secret chamber without being seen. The base of the central pier is surrounded by shelves forming a buffet; on great occasions the magnificent treasures of ancient gold and silver plate and vessels from the royal household were displayed here.

At the end of the fifteenth century Tsar Ivan III began to plan new living quarters for himself. The foundation for this palace was laid in 1499; the work was supervised by the architect Alevisio Novy, who had previously demonstrated his abilities in the construction of religious edifices. These living quarters, constituting the lower floors of the still existing Teremnoi Dvorets, were finished in 1508 after the death of Ivan. During the construction of the palace, work also proceeded on a masonry wall to protect the palace from the constantly menacing Tatars.

Masonry Structures

The experimenting with wooden building forms and their adaptation and incorporation in the masonry architecture of Novgorod and Pskov went on in a leisurely manner for a long time, but in early sixteenth-century Moscow this process speeded up. In the suburbs of Moscow a number of memorial and votive churches appeared in rapid succession, and many of the wooden forms were reflected with increasing boldness. In looking about for sources of inspiration, the Moscow architects turned to the indigenous forms of wooden church architecture, with the result that early in the sixteenth century came the substitution of the wooden tent tower for the traditional Byzantine cupola. The influence exerted by wooden architecture also brought about a number of other important changes: increased emphasis on height; introduction of entrance porches and the use of external galleries; combination of the pyramidal spire with the cupola; and the introduction of separate free-standing belfries.

The Church of the Ascension at Kolomenskoe, erected in 1530–32 by Vasili III, presents an important step in the process of transition from alien to national form. Here the most characteristic and most expressive of national wooden architectural forms—the tent—was incorporated, for the first time, into ecclesiastical masonry architecture. The architect succeeded not only in translating the wooden forms, but also in imparting to them the poignant feeling of national architecture. The whole building has the firmness and compactness of a monolithic pyramid, recalling the form of the great wooden tent churches. There is the same foundation course of the arcaded porches, the same cruciform plan, the same octagonal central element, and the same tentlike pyramid. The kinship of this masonry structure to the wooden churches of the north is quite evident. Although its elements were gathered from a variety of sources, they are fused and transfigured into national substance.

Probably the most striking monument of this period is the Church of Basil the Blessed (*Vasili Blazhenny*, 1553–60)— best known in the West of all Russian churches for its marked difference from Western tradition. It occupies an exceptional place in Russian architecture and deserves to be considered at length. This boldest departure from classic or Byzantine architecture violates the academic laws of symmetry and proportion as understood by the Western world, and the structure is uniquely medieval Russian in content, form, technique, decoration, and feeling.

Long the subject of heated discussions, the architecture of St. Basil's has been either greatly ridiculed and termed "the dream of a diseased imagination" or highly praised as a unique expression of the medieval Russian genius. Theophile Gautier compared the agglomeration of its many elements to the crystals of a giant madrepore. Other Western observers, notably the French De Gustine and the German Blazius, described its ensemble of towers and cupolas as "a bush, a plant, or a bouquet of varicolored flowers." However it strikes the beholder, there is no denying that, in spite of its seemingly incongruous jumble of architectural elements and decorative details, the church is uniquely original in conception, design, and execution. Furthermore, some observers believe that the architecture of the church, in its departure from the traditional plan and distribution of masses of the Kremlin cathedrals, reflected the beginning of the new, national epoch in Russian art—an expression of the aesthetics of the rising middle classes and no longer that of the dwellers inside the Kremlin, the formerly powerful boyars. Its very location on Red Square points to the steadily growing importance of the districts beyond the Kremlin.

These varying views and the paradoxical strangeness of the structure can perhaps be better understood in the light of the historical circumstances surrounding its construction. As previously indicated, the epoch of Ivan the Terrible, during which St. Basil's was built, was marked by diligent searchings and experimentations in many phases of art. The native architects, in their attempt to break with the alien form of Byzantine traditions, turned for inspiration to the indigenous forms of wooden churches. The graceful, slender tent roofs, the chapels, galleries, and porches with their picturesque stairways, the *kokoshniki, bochki,* and onion-shaped cupolas—all these distinctive features of the wooden churches captivated the imagination of the local contemporary builders.

The Church of St. Basil the Blessed, originally known as the Cathedral of the Intercession of the Virgin (*Pokrovsky Sobor*), is a votive church built by Ivan IV in commemoration of the conquest of Kazan and Astrakhan. At that time Russia was passing through a particularly intense phase of religious fervor. The Stoglav Council had recently met; the young Tsar, flushed with victory, wanted to signalize his military success as a triumph of the Cross over Islam.

At the suggestion of the Metropolitan Makari, Ivan decided to erect a masonry church dedicated to the Intercession (*Pokrov*) of the Virgin. Because this was to be a memorial church, easy of access to all of the people of Moscow, Ivan decided on a site on Red Square at the edge of the ditch along the Kremlin. With the church as the central, dominant element, he planned eight smaller but separate churches (not chapels) of wood, each with its own altar and iconostasis, dedicated to a saint whose feast day coincided with one of the days of the eight decisive victories over the Tatars. These temporary wooden churches were later replaced by masonry. In 1588 another church was added on the northeast side of the cathedral to house the crypt of Basil the Blessed. One of the most venerated altars in the church—the third in importance—was dedicated to the entry of Jesus into Jerusalem. Foreign visitors to Moscow during the seventeenth century were impressed with the colorful Palm Sunday (*Verbnoe Voskresen'ye*) processions, and referred to St. Basil's as the Church of Jerusalem.

St. Basil, for whom this extraordinary church was named, was a popular mendicant prophet and miracle worker of the sixteenth century who claimed as his distinctive glory that he was "idiotic for Christ's sake." This church contains relics of another saint—John the Idiot—as well as the chain and cross worn in penance by St. Basil. Idiocy was a common form of religious fervor in Russia, and these dedicated idiots (*urodivyie*) were treated with reverence.

Begun in 1553, St. Basil's was finished and consecrated in 1560. It was designed by the Russian architects Barma and Posnik Yakovlev, who, in the words of the chronicler, were "very wise and eminently fit for this marvelous work." According to a persistent legend, the Church of St. Basil was designed by an Italian architect, who was then blinded by order of the Tsar so that the Italian would not be able to produce a more beautiful church elsewhere. Another version of the same legend says that the Tsar asked the architect if he could build an even finer, more magnificent church. When the architect replied that he could, the Tsar ordered him beheaded so that St. Basil's would remain an unrivaled monument.

The St. Basil group of churches is basically cross-shaped, the arms of the cross extending from a square center—the main church—over which rises the central tower covered with a tent-shaped roof and crowned with a gilt cupola. At each arm of the cross, along the principal axes, is an octagonal church. Four other secondary churches (two square and two of irregular outline) are along the diagonal axes. All these elements are placed over a tall, vaulted substructure—the typical lower story of the Russian wooden churches. The pyramidal belfry at the southeast corner is separated from the church. The plan and the general massing of the elements are unusual not only in the accepted concept of church design, but in the distribution of the main masses. Rather than being merely the result of some fanciful caprice, the arrangement and grouping were probably planned by Metropolitan Makari.

The main church is of stone and brick and covered with stucco. In the seventeenth century the entire structure, originally white, was painted in variegated colors, the stairways were roofed over, the sheet iron covering of the cupolas was replaced by tile, and the old belfry was replaced by the present tent-roofed bell tower.

Like the church at Kolomenskoe, St. Basil's embodies the characteristic architectural features of the wooden churches of northeastern Russia translated into masonry. Here too the transition from the square substructure to the main octagonal tower is accomplished by recessive, interspaced tiers of ornate *kokoshniki*. The same method is used to form the transition from the massive base to a smaller octagon supporting the tent-shaped spire surmounted by a small bulbous cupola. The eleven steeples are banded together like an immense bundle of fantastically shaped plants. The eight cupolas, dominated by the central pyramid, are all of the same general silhouette but are different in design—as if to single out each of the component churches in the complex. Some, with their twisted, variegated shapes, are reminiscent of oriental turbans; some are decorated with ribbed or interlacing designs; others are faceted, giving them the appearance of pineapples; still another has imbrications reminiscent of the aspen shingles of the wooden churches. All the cupolas are bulbous, projecting considerably beyond the diameter of the drum. This diversity of forms and decorative features is further heightened by the lavish use of colored tile.

The interior is by contrast somber and cavernous. It produces the impression that the church was sculptured from one huge block of stone. Each of the nine church chambers is prolonged upward in a kind of drum surmounted by a dome. The chambers, suggestive of ancient frescoed catacombs, are connected by low, vaulted passages within the thick walls, with a narrow, vaulted corridor around them. The low, arched doorways and windows are of various forms, all deeply recessed and flanked with engaged columns. The interior of the central church was frescoed in 1784 during the reign of Catherine II; the other surrounding churches were frescoed between 1839 and 1845.

St. Basil's is understandably strange, puzzling to Western eyes; yet it was well suited to the age and its former surroundings. It still exercises a singular attraction at all times of the year, but is especially fascinating in winter. Seen in the pale sunshine, with its clump of pinnacles and cupolas illuminated against the sky, the building is most impressive.

The sixteenth century produced not only a series of significant works, but perfected new construction methods, types and forms of multi-columned and tent churches, large architectural ensembles of the fortress-monastery type, and formal audience chambers, paving the way for formal civil architecture, whose influence on the subsequent development of Russian art is significant. Toward the end of the sixteenth century a special state organization, the Bureau of Masonry Works, was established. The intensive building activities evolved new architectural ideas and types, incorporating and transmuting the attainments of ancient Russian building.

The Time of Trouble, the Civil War, and the social up-heavals that marked the beginning of the seventeenth century put a stop to Moscow's intense building activities for a few years. The city was plundered and almost razed to the ground, but despite the terrible devastation, Moscow began to build itself anew with surprising rapidity. The old tradition of putting up ready-hewn log houses very quickly eliminated the housing shortage. After they had finished the necessary repairs of the Kremlin walls and cathedrals, the Moscow rulers began to think of more serious work. It is significant that one of their first undertakings was the remodeling and ornamentation of the towers and main gates to the Kremlin.

It was during this period that the extensive reconstruction and enlargement of the old Terem Palace took place. The new palace is a brick structure; the window architraves, portals, entablatures, and parapets are of white stone covered with carved strapwork, foliage, and figures of beasts and birds painted in bright colors. The ornamentation dates from the sixteenth and seventeenth centuries; it was renovated in the early nineteenth century. The apartments, contained within a five-story structure (now forming the north side of the Kremlin Grand Palace) are a series of small, low, generally vaulted rooms decorated with polychrome ornaments and images painted on gold or other backgrounds.

In the reign of Tsar Aleksei (1645–76) the old palace attained its most beautiful and luxurious aspect. The five apartments of the fourth story were renovated and refurnished as his private quarters. The first room functioned as a waiting room for the boyars seeking audience with the Tsar. The second room, the Room of the Cross, served as a reception room for the Tsar and occasionally for boyar councils. The third room, sometimes called the Golden, was the

Tsar's study, where the high officials of state were received. This room contained a dais for the throne and some benches along the walls, where the boyars were seated according to seniority. The center window of the Golden Room, known as the Petitioners' Window, had a device for raising and lowering a small box between the room and the ground. Into this box the poor and the wronged could place their petitions and complaints addressed directly to the Tsar. The next room, the Tsar's bedroom, has a carved four-poster with curtains of brocade and silk. Along its walls are benches upholstered in Venetian velvet. The fifth room was the Tsar's private chapel or oratory, which has a pulpit with a fourteenth-century illuminated manuscript of the Book of the Gospels.

Outstanding as decorative features in all these rooms are the great faïence tile stoves. The stoves in the Tsar's study and in the chapel are especially noteworthy as monuments to the great skill and artistry of the seventeenth-century Russian craftsmen in producing colored and glazed tiles and pottery.

Back of these rooms is a long narrow corridor with a carved stone floor. According to tradition, this corridor served as the inspection place for girls eligible to become the Tsar's bride. On appointed days the most beautiful daughters of the best families would be lined up in this corridor; the Tsar, walking slowly up and down, would look them over three times, and when his "luminous" eyes fell upon the most desirable he would present her with a specially embroidered towel as a token of his favor.

The fifth floor or "penthouse" apartment has heavily ornamented vault webbing, pendant keys, door entablatures, window frames, and colored tile stoves.

This remnant of the past is a labyrinth of low corridors and vaulted chambers adorned with barbaric magnificence. The few extant architectural and decorative elements are truly authentic remains of medieval Russian art. Except for a few modern details and perhaps well-meant but unfortunate restorations, these chambers offer a complete picture of the art and environmental culture of the royal court of the late seventeenth century.

The furniture and accessories remained practically unchanged from the death of Tsar Feodor in 1682 until the restoration of 1830. Then much of the feeling of antiquity was destroyed, giving these chambers a somewhat artificial toylike appearance, but there is still a strong seventeenth-century aura about them.

The decoration of the exterior of the Teremnoi Dvorets is in some ways even more striking than the interior. Alongside the Western classical decorative elements are ornamental motifs of a decidedly Russian folk character, especially in the windows and the entrance portals, that are the most interesting decorative details of the Terem façades. The builders of the palace embellished them with luxurious carving—the motifs borrowed from the wooden *khoromy* of the tsar—and thus transformed them into highly individual creations.

Among the seventeenth-century palaces in the Kremlin is the one that belonged to the boyar Ilia Miloslavsky, who first occupied it in 1651. When Miloslavsky died, Tsar Aleksei Mikhailovich remodeled it into a theater. Known as Poteshnyi Dvorets (Amusement Palace), it still exists, though it has been considerably changed. Its projecting cantilevered balcony, especially constructed to support a house chapel, is particularly interesting.

Between 1680 and 1690 many gardens, balconies, and stairways were added to the Kremlin. Near the Church of the
Saviour Behind the Golden Grille, stone passageways, covered and open arcades, hanging gardens, and cupolas crowning the roofs of various chapels were built—the passages and
galleries permitting the tsar to communicate with the patriarch without having to leave cover. During these years, when
the ancient and traditional forms merged harmoniously with
the elements of the early Moscow baroque, the Kremlin
reached its mature beauty.

Following the example of the Tsar, who had reconstructed
the Terem and Poteshnyi palaces in the Kremlin, the nobility, the important officials, and the rich merchants also began
to build for themselves masonry mansions and chapels.
These structures show the gradual evolution of the style of
the earlier wooden palaces and churches.

The basic structural forms of the Moscow churches were
fully developed in the sixteenth century. It remained for the
next century to concentrate its efforts on the refinement of
these forms and on the embellishment of the façades with
opulent ornamentation. We see the "tent" spires degenerate
into mere decoration; they are used as exterior ornamented
features and are set loosely in numbers over gabled roofs and
on top of roof vaulting. This decorative use of the formerly
functional element is combined with the liberal employment
of the other sixteenth-century structural device—the *kokoshniki*. These, in retreating and ascending tiers, are used as a
decorative screen for the drumlike bases of the spires, and
sometimes as parapets over the cornices.

Church building had settled down to a tacit acceptance
of the pentacupolar church as dictated by Patriarch Nikon,

but it never relinquished the pyramidal tent form. The architects of Moscow resorted to some ruses in order to circumvent the clerical ban on this favorite roof form. They made clever use of the permission granted by the clergy to erect tents over church annexes, that is, over porches and bell towers. These tent roofs over the bell towers present the final and perfected stage in the development of this national roof feature. The variety of forms and the manner with which the Russian builders played with retreating and over-lapping *kokoshniki*, with arrangement and grouping of cupolas and tents during the sixteenth and seventeenth centuries forms one of the enchanting chapters in the history of Russian architecture.

In the details and ornamentation of the Muscovite churches Byzantine elements began to give way to a less severe and more picturesque style. The façades began to be treated with a view primarily to pictorial effect. Ornament became profuse, varied, and independent of structural logic. By the last third of the seventeenth century the vogue for rich embellishment reached its zenith. Polychromy asserted itself; colored and glazed tile and carved stone ornament used in combination with brick patterns were employed extensively. Some of the wall panels of that period are so intricately and beautifully carved as to produce the effect of exquisite stone lacework.

Muscovite architecture became what Western critics like to describe as exotic and what the Russian art historians of today prefer to designate as "Moscow or Naryshkin Baroque." Baroque ideas found a fertile soil in Moscow and gave fresh vigor to its architecture. They strengthened the existing decorative tendencies, but also quickened the constructive imagination and gave new life to the spirit that had evolved the tent form. The last remains of the severe Byzantine style went overboard, and Muscovite architecture was free to revel in constructive and pictorial freedom.

Moscow or Naryshkin Baroque

The Italian Renaissance at its height overflowed to other lands, but missed Russia. Its impact on Russian architecture took place mainly in its very early and very late (Baroque) phases. The first phase of the Renaissance reflected itself primarily in various architectural details and techniques, changing and improving the methods of construction. It hardly touched the building forms then strongly in favor. On the other hand, the late phase of the Renaissance had an enormous influence and brought about the creation of entirely new building types. This architectural style—manifesting itself as a new power to mold space and to produce a unified whole from the most diverse elements—was probably the most international of all styles. Its expression in some countries revealed itself in almost an absence of specific regional characteristics; everywhere there was a uniformity in architectural devices and details.

Russia, however, was able to assimilate and refashion this style into types entirely individual to herself. One reason for this, Grabar points out, is that the Baroque appeared on the Russian scene suddenly, as it were, and not as the result of a protracted process of evolution. Further, Moscow received the motifs of the new style not in their pristine forms, directly from the West, but in a roundabout way, from the South, from the Ukraine, which in turn received them from Poland and Lithuania. The Baroque of the Ukraine, though undoubtedly a provincialized version of the universal style, has many local peculiarities, and even its brash pomposity is infused with a distinctly indigenous flavor.

Moscow also received from the Ukraine the type of peculiar wooden tent church in which the tent pyramid consists not of one continuous octagonal cone, gradually narrowing to a point, but is a structure composed of a series of octagonal prisms gradually diminishing in size and culminating in small cupolas. This type was translated from wood into stone, and out of its elements a new unique style was evolved and became known as the "Moscow" or "Naryshkin Baroque." In some ways this mode, though short-lived, is one of the brightest phenomena of Russian architecture.

Its outstanding characteristics are a rather unique application of brick and white stone in the decoration of façades; an extraordinary felicity and nobility of architectural ornament; and a classic simplicity and clarity of composition with an almost fairy-tale wealth of detail, often of foreign derivation but imaginatively transformed into a clearly expressed national style. In a little over twenty-five years this style developed, grew to maturity, and achieved a finish and a distinct flavor which is still the marvel and pride of Muscovy.

One of the most delightful examples of this style is the Church of the Intercession of the Holy Virgin at Fili, the estate of the boyar Naryshkin in Moscow. This graceful structure was conceived and executed in 1693 with such perfection that only very few other structures (the Church at Nerl near Vladimir and some of the churches and belfries in Novgorod) can be mentioned as its rivals. To quote Grabar: "Everything about this church, from top to bottom, is matchless; its plan, the very enticing idea of the sweep of its widely extended grand stairways leading to large terraces out of which rises the body of the church, its finely perceived, carefully studied, elegant, and well-proportioned silhouette, and the lacy belts that crown its walls; everywhere and in everything there is the hand of a great poet and an architect-magician." The church is placed on an elevated terrace-like substructure. An open gallery served by three monumental stairways surrounds the four-lobed base. Over the base rises a series of octagonal prisms, diminishing in size and leading up to a small terminal cupola. The central element is surrounded by semicircular appurtenances, one of which serves as a sanctuary, the others as vestibules or narthexes. The general silhouette is reminiscent of the stately Church of the Ascension at Kolomenskoe.

The style was mainly patronized by the Naryshkins. They were well acquainted with the various manifestations of the baroque and contributed much to its cultivation—hence the name, "Naryshkin Baroque." The church embodies many elements of this style in its interior, which is almost as rich in ornament as the exterior. The iconostasis and the pulpit are finely carved and brilliantly decorated.

It is interesting to contrast the delightful church of Fili with another church built in the same decade, the Church of the Miracle of the Virgin at Dubrovitsy near Moscow, built in 1690–1704 by Prince Vasili Golitsyn. It is a white stone structure on a four-lobed base. The tower, which is completely covered with elaborate carving, looks like a piece of sculptured ivory. The architecture of the church typifies the state of mind of many of the Europe-oriented members of the nobility at the time Peter the Great came to the throne.

The striking interior and exterior opulence of this church, where formal religious sculpture appears for the first time in a Russian church, is explained by the whimsy of an impetuous and self-indulging Europe-worshiping prince, who, probably abetted by the Tsar himself, dared to introduce such innovations and break the centuries-long traditions of Russian church architecture. Its lavish and meticulously carved decorations, in their novelty and sumptuousness, are reminiscent of the French decorative devices of the sixteenth century. French mannerisms are especially noticeable in the rusticated monumental substructure, and in the playfully worked architraves and settings of the dormer windows. It was an extremely expensive, striking, and daring structure, and, in its day, it created much heated discussion and aroused the sullen, if silent, resentment of the clergy. Yet every noble-man of the period was envious and anxious to adorn his estate with a church of somewhat the same style.

CHAPTER FIVE

THE MOSCOW SCHOOL OF PAINTING

THE aesthetic culture of Muscovite Russia in the age of nationalism is best reflected in the art of that period. It was a religious art, guided by reverence for ecclesiastical tradition, yet strongly influenced by the native arts of the Russian people, especially in the sphere of religious painting.

From the tenth century until the end of the seventeenth century painting was virtually confined to icon painting, an art introduced to Kievan Russia from Byzantium. Both in Byzantium and in Russia this art was limited to the representation of the Deity, sacred personages, and scriptural events; it was never an attempt to achieve realism or authentic portraiture. The fundamental principle of this art is a pictorial expression of church doctrine, to represent sacred events and indicate their meaning. Being primarily an object of veneration and an auxiliary to worship, the icon was as formalized as the sequence of the liturgy or the ritual of a sacrament. Nevertheless, despite strict rules governing their painting, icons exhibit a variety of styles, subjects, compositional characteristics, and moods. In spite of the devoutness with which the Russian icon painters regarded their Byzantine models, they contrived to give them a popular appeal, in both line and color.

The style and manner of Byzantium spread from Kiev to the northern centers, where the influence persisted for several centuries. The twelfth century was a period of copying and assimilating Byzantine principles and forms; as early as the thirteenth century these began to assume a Russian aspect. By the last quarter of the fourteenth century the borrowed art forms had become unmistakably national.

The search for a solution of the religious problems connected with icon painting and for greater freedom in interpreting the principles of the Byzantine style were important factors in forming local artistic groups. The new cultural and political centers—Vladimir-Suzdal and Novgorod—became the starting points of artistic deviation, developing the legacy of Kiev, each region along its own lines, thus laying the foundation of several schools.

The Novgorodians treated the Byzantine patterns with great independence, and as early as the thirteenth century their work showed unmistakable national characteristics. The severity of faces is softened, composition is simplified, the silhouette becomes bold and ever more important, and the palette is lightened by bright cinnabar, emerald-green, and lemon-yellow tones. The rigid Byzantine patterns with dark colors and austere lines become graceful, bright, and less solemn. The artists of Vladimir-Suzdal showed greater restraint. The influence of the classic Byzantine works of the eleventh and twelfth centuries was still all-powerful, inclining them to be very cautious in their departure from tradition. The Vladimir School, therefore, and the Moscow School, which superseded it in the fourteenth century, differ from other schools by a closer adherence to their Byzantine prototypes, their reverent preservation for a longer time.

Moscow, which had appeared on the historical scene relatively late, did not have her own original artistic culture in the twelfth century. She had to make use of the accumulated heritage of the older Russian cities, and it was only natural that she would first adhere to the traditions of the Vladimir-Suzdal Principality to which she had long been closely tied. The absence of early monuments prevents us from tracing the first independent steps in the development of the Moscow School of painting. The frequent raids of the Tatars had systematically destroyed much that was of cultural value. The oldest archives of the principality, the rare manuscripts, icons, and the costly liturgical furnishings that, in the words of the chronicler, "filled the Moscow churches to the rafters" were all put to the torch in 1382 by the Tatar General Tokhtamysh.

But late in the fourteenth century came a change that was the beginning of the flowering of Moscow art. Moscow emissaries visited Constantinople frequently, and a wave of Greek and southern Slavonic influence came over Russia. It was partly connected with the immigration of many Serbian and Bulgarian clerics fleeing the Turks, who had just put an end to the independence of their countries. Many Greek artists settled in Novgorod and Moscow, and a number of Byzantine works of the Palaeologue Renaissance were brought into Russia. In these years, Moscow also manifested a lively interest in the renowned older works of art. In 1395 the famous icon, *The Vladimir Mother of God*, considered to be the *Palladium* of Russia, was installed in the Cathedral of the Assumption in the Kremlin. This icon was destined to play an important role in the development of Russian painting, serving as a model for the iconographic type of Virgin known as *Umilenie* (Our Lady of Tenderness). It represents the conception in Russian iconography of the Virgin and

127

Child as an intimate and tender group with nothing of that awe-inspiring austerity met so often in the eastern part of the Byzantine world.

Moscow icon painting was developing under the best conditions and auspices. To begin with, it derived from the Vladimir-Suzdal School, which for the early period stood highest in artistic skill, traditions, and aims. Later, when icon painting in Russia began really to flourish, Moscow benefited by the best artists and the best models from the developed schools of Novgorod and Pskov. Novgorod and Moscow experienced the influence of the final brilliant stage of the Palaeologue Renaissance, reaching its highest point in the last quarter of the fourteenth century. This is particularly reflected in the works of the celebrated Theophanes the Greek who migrated to Russia about 1370. He seems to have fallen in love with the country of his adoption and assimilated many of its characteristics. As in the case of his great compatriot, the artist Domenico Theotocópuli (1541–1614), surnamed El Greco, whose long stay in Toledo, Spain, made him a typical representative of Spanish art, Theophanes' artistic genius reached its highest development in Russia. He esablished his reputation as a great icon painter in Novgorod in the 1370's. In the middle of the 1390's he was invited to Moscow, where he and his Russian assistants decorated the interior of the Church of the Nativity of the Virgin. In 1399 he was working again with his pupils in the old Cathedral of Archangel Michael. In 1405, assisted by the Elder Prokhor from Gorodets and by Andrei Rublev, he executed the iconostasis for the Cathedral of the Annunciation in the Moscow Kremlin. To Theophanes himself may be ascribed the most important tier of the iconostasis—the enthroned Christ flanked by the Virgin and John the Precursor, and the figures of archangels, apostles, and other saints. The figures are tall, somewhat severe, with dark faces and long thin arms, sustained in rich contrasting tones, full of subdued pathos. These paintings are marked by a close adherence to Byzantine standards of the fourteenth century, but their highly original style places them beyond the bounds of Byzantine art.

The artistic interests of late fourteenth-century Moscow were not limited exclusively to Byzantine art. Her artists became familiar with the works of the southern Slavs. Moreover, by this time Moscow had its own well-established tradition and its cadre of artists who approached problems in their own way. The Byzantine tradition underwent its first vital transformation on Russian soil. In Moscow this movement culminated in that great artist Andrei Rublev.

Rublev (*ca.* 1360–1430), the most significant figure among Russian icon painters, was a monk of the Trinity and St. Sergius Monastery near Moscow, where he probably received his artistic training. Later he was transferred to the Spas Andronikov Monastery (now the Rublev Museum) in Moscow, where he spent the rest of his life. It was the time when Moscow, rapidly forging ahead to the very front of the disunited and feuding Russian principalities, took the lead in the struggle against the Tatars. The Mongol defeat on the field of Kulikovo resulted in an upsurge in national consciousness and vastly increased the political importance of the Moscow Principality.

The decisive years in Rublev's creative growth were the 1390's, when Moscow was fast becoming a major cultural center exposed to all the latest trends of Byzantine and Serbian art. It is highly probable that Rublev had the opportunity to study the work of Theophanes, the leading figure in Moscow art circles. Although Rublev's aesthetic ideals were entirely different from those of the Greek master, the impassioned images of Theophanes' saints must have made a deep impression on the younger artist. It was probably Theophanes who introduced him to the latest trends in Byzantine art, enlarged his color range, taught him new composition devices, and prepared him for the creation of the classic form of the Russian iconostasis.

Traces of his first activities as a mature artist can be seen in Zvenigorod. Here are his early works (the frescoes of the Assumption Cathedral and the icons of the iconostasis in the Cathedral of the Nativity) which throw light on his creative development. Most of his later artistic activities are closely connected with Moscow and its nearby cities and monasteries. He decorated the walls of the cathedrals of the Annunciation at Moscow (1405) and the Assumption at Vladimir (1408) with frescoes. But the best known of his paintings is the icon, *The Old Testament Trinity*, painted about 1411 for the iconostasis of the Trinity and St. Sergius Monastery. (At present this icon is in the Tretyakov Gallery, Moscow.) The subject—the visit of the three angels to Abraham and Sarah—was popular in Byzantine art. In this icon the severe symbolism of the Byzantine tradition has been transformed into something more intimately human. The angels acquire an aspect of gentle grace and supernatural luminosity. In the beauty of the colors, the spirituality of the faces, and the quiet concentration expressed in the three figures we can observe a distinct non-Byzantine feeling, but even more important is the novel, peculiarly Russian mood of dreamy sublimation. Rublev's *Trinity* is one of the great creations of medieval Russian painting. In it we have the unearthliness that is the icon's highest merit.

The icons of the Festival tier from the Annunciation Cathedral, the *Last Judgment*, and a few other works are attributed to Rublev. A great similarity to his style appears also in the big half-figure paintings of a *deësis* (the image of the Saviour between the Virgin Mary and John the Precursor) discovered by chance in a state of semi-destruction in a storehouse of the Zvenigorod Cathedral. The few authentic works of Rublev help one to realize the degree of independence attained by fifteenth-century Russian art. Prior to Rublev, Moscow painting was devoid of a clearly defined individuality. It expressed a struggle between two sharply differing trends. The Byzantine current was stubbornly resisting the native Russian. Rublev was the very first to change this condition. While utilizing the Byzantine legacy, he transformed it. To quote Lazarev: "Rublev definitely broke with the Byzantine severity and asceticism. From the Byzantine legacy he extracted its antique Hellenistic core and freed it from all the later ascetic stratifications. His art is gentler, more poetic and luminous than that of his predecessors. The pigments of his palette are derived not from the traditional color canons, but from his native landscape. His wonderful blues are suggested by the blue of the spring sky; his whites are reminiscent of the whites of the Russian birch trees; his green color is close to the color of unripe rye; his golden ochre recalls the colors of fallen autumn leaves; and in his dark green colors there is something of the duskiness of the Russian coniferous forest."

He is justly considered the founder of the Moscow School of painting, whose influence ranged far afield; it was powerful with his contemporaries and endured long after his death, making the fifteenth century the golden age of the Russian icon. Rublev was beatified by the Russian Orthodox church, one of the very few artists ever to be numbered among the saints.

It was during Rublev's time that the peculiarly Russian decorative ensemble of icons known as the iconostasis was formulated and became characteristic of the Muscovite church. Novgorod, Pskov, and Vladimir-Suzdal all contributed, in various degrees, to the development of the iconostasis, but it was at Moscow, in the persons of Theophanes the Greek, Prokhor of Gorodets, Andrei Rublev, and Daniil Chernyi, that its classical form was evolved and perfected.

The iconostasis is the screen or partition separating the sanctuary, where the sacrament of the Eucharist is celebrated, from the nave, where the congregation stands. It serves as a frame and background for the many icons which are arranged in tiers in a traditionally prescribed manner. Iconostases in the form of a barrier between the sanctuary and the rest of the church existed in Byzantine churches from ancient times. The form and height of these barriers varied. Sometimes they were solid low marble walls or balustrades; at other times they were high latticed screens or arcades. The sanctuary barrier of the Justinian era (527–65), a colonnade surmounted by an architrave, began to grow more complex very early. At first, the architrave was embellished by carved religious symbols—usually a cross. Towards the end of the ninth century half-length figures of Christ flanked by saints began to be put upon the architrave. These icons were usually painted on a wooden panel, which the Greeks called *"templon."* This Byzantine form of the sanctuary barrier was adopted by the Russians from the Greeks, but the Russians gradually transformed it by increasing the number of icons and tiers. The ancient *templon*, the triptych containing the figure of Christ was renamed *"Deisus"* (a corruption of the

Greek word *deësis*, meaning prayer or supplication). This composition came to embody the idea of intercession by the Virgin and John the Precursor beseeching the Saviour to forgive the sins of humanity.

The gradual evolution and enrichment of the iconostasis took place in the Vladimir-Suzdal and Novgorod regions during the thirteenth and fourteenth centuries. In Moscow, by the fifteenth century, it had reached an impressive multi-tiered height, each tier containing a specified assortment of icons. Its form was to become classic for many generations. Definite positions were assigned to certain iconic subjects, and the icons were arranged in five (occasionally seven) tiers. Their disposition was indicated by the church fathers, primarily with an eye to the inherent symbolic significance of the various subjects and their visual storytelling impact upon the worshipers. The complex iconography of the church dogma—the Revelation, Incarnation, and Redemption—formerly depicted by the mosaics of the central dome, and drum apse and by the wall frescoes—was gradually incorporated in the iconostasis and its central doors. The Pantocrator, the prophets, and forefathers were transferred from the dome to the Prophets' and Forefathers' Tiers; the Church Festivals, from the vaults and walls to the Holiday Tiers; the *deësis*, from the central apse to the Deësis Tier; the evangelists, from the pendentives to the central or Royal Doors through which only the officiating priest and tsar might enter the sanctuary.

As an ensemble, the iconostasis provided a visual record of church history, moving from the Old Testament patriarchs and prophets in the upper tier to the local saints in the lowest tier. Most interesting is the way in which the Muscovite artists united the symbolic theme of the iconostasis with a purely decorative function. They developed and expanded the traditional Byzantine image of the *deësis*, placing these three panels in the center above the Royal Doors and treating them as the nucleus of the composition. On the right and left, they added two archangels, two apostles, two fathers of the church, and two martyrs, a sequence of majestic figures forming the *chin* (the range of archangels, saints, and church fathers flanking the central *deësis*) converging towards the center of the iconostasis and detaching themselves as slender silhouettes on a golden or bright-colored background. The surviving iconostasis of the Cathedral of the Annunciation in the Moscow Kremlin—with its huge figures of the *chin* (forty by eighty inches) and the extensive cycle of the church festivals—marked the birth of the classical form of the Russian iconostasis and prepared the ground for those of the Assumption Cathedral in Vladimir and in the Trinity St. Sergius Monastery. Their richness of color and beauty of composition are superb examples of pre-Petrine art.

The iconostasis was addressed to a large, mixed, mostly illiterate congregation. It demanded the development of a special art form which would provide a thorough integration of a large number of figures, each preserving its individuality but all woven into a single unit. The height of the structure prompted the artist to outline the figures, other than the representation of the festivals, in a monumental style with a clear-cut silhouette. This vigorous portrayal of figures influenced the treatment of smaller icons—preserving the elongated proportion of the figures, the simplification of the color scheme, and the general pattern. The design of the iconostasis, together with the number and disposition of its various elements, remained for a long time the principal theme of the Moscow School of painting. It created a vogue for complex icons whose composition contained crowds resembling an iconostasis. The complex type of icon with its conventional hieratic images had to relate graphically episodes from the Holy Scriptures, the lives of the saints, the meaning of holidays; in fact, all that might interest the pious but illiterate man in the domain of religion. Thus the icon became the Bible for the masses.

Icon painting continued to flourish throughout the fifteenth century. There was, moreover, an ever increasing demand for icons, especially small ones, from the Moscow nobility and the wealthy merchants, for use in private chapels. The vast masses of the population were also aspiring to have icons in their homes, several if possible, since each image of the Virgin or of some particularly revered saint was believed to possess its own supernatural powers and protection. One could hardly have too many. The icon became an inseparable companion of the Orthodox Russian from birth to death, and it was used to impart blessings on all significant events. It was transmitted as a family heirloom through generations or presented as a precious gift to the church. It became usual then to place an icon in the far right-hand corner of each room, as well as at the head of each bed in the house.

The outstanding icon painter of the second half of the fifteenth century was Dionysius (Dionisi, *ca.* 1440–1508). His artistic activities coincide with the period of centralization of the Russian state, when Moscow experienced a great political and cultural upsurge and her art began to acquire an all-Russian character. It was during this time that the numerous Russian monasteries became centers of commerce and industry, possessors of vast lands and great wealth. Thus the entire mode of monastic life acquired a more worldly character, reflected in the ecclesiastical art of the period.

Dionysius' paintings are marked by the extreme elongated stylizing of his figures combined with a subtle design. His manner of presentation reveals the interest he felt in the technical aspects of painting, especially composition. In 1480 with three of his co-workers (Pope Timothy, Yarets, and Kon) he was invited to Moscow to execute an iconostasis for the Cathedral of the Assumption, just completed by Fioravanti. In 1484, Paisi the Elder and Dionysius, with his sons Theodosius (Feodor) and Vladimir, painted an extensive series of icons for the Monastery of Volokolamsk. In 1500–1502 he was working with his sons in the Monastery of St. Therapont on the White Lake. The frescoes of the Church of the Nativity of the Virgin in this monastery, executed late in his life, are unquestionably his greatest achievement—truly superb monuments of Russian pre-Petrine art.

Like that of the icon painters of the Rublev period, Dionysius' work was done in collaboration with a team of co-workers. The chroniclers, in recording certain works, usually mention his name with the names of several others. We have few specimens of easel painting which can be with certainty ascribed to his brush; but we can be fairly sure of at least three such works: two large icons of the Moscow metropolitans, St. Peter and St. Aleksei, and an icon of the Crucifixion; they have all the earmarks of the famous master, who loved tall, slender figures with small heads, rhythmic lines, and delicate coloring.

The work of Dionysius represents the creative searchings of the fifteenth century at their height, and at the same time opens up a new era. There is much in his work that is closely related to the classic period of Russian icon painting, but there is in it also a foreshadowing of the beginning of the crisis in the artistic ideals of the Rublev era. Dionysius played an important role in the history of medieval Russian art. By following the path indicated by Rublev but at the same time exercising his own genius, he immortalized the art of his predecessor and made it the common property of all the Russian people. With Dionysius the splendorous, festive, exultant art of Moscow became the leading trend in Russia. It began to be accepted as a standard by provincial art schools and imitated everywhere.

By the middle of the sixtenth century the Tatar yoke had been cast off, and the last remnants of independence of the various detached principalities had gradually come to an end. The Moscow Kremlin became the center of the artistic life of the country. Here, at the tsar's court, the activities of the state's best architects, artists, designers, scribes, engravers, and craftsmen were concentrated. Work was being carried on directly under the supervision of the metropolitan and the tsar. Icon painters were first summoned to Moscow to participate in the unprecedented activity of building and decorating the cathedrals and churches by the palace. Scribes, illuminators, and engravers were gathered to compile and illustrate the huge folios of the Nikonian Chronicles and other literary works. These artists, writers, and craftsmen brought with them their individual tastes and their local traditions. The stronger and more individualistic masters combined the principles inherited from Byzantium and those surviving from Novgorod with purely decorative and graphic principles whose roots lay in Russian peasant art. Especially during the second half of the sixteenth century, icon painting is found more and more to contain character-istics of rustic art and themes from real life.

This evolution first became noticeable in the gradual elim-ination of the Hellenistic setting of the icon—landscape and architecture. Greek basilicas with their porticoes and atria were replaced by the tent-shaped roofs and onion-bulb cupolas of Russian churches. The white walls of these churches and their architectural forms furnished a new ornamental motif. Moreover, many icons now began to represent native Russian saints and episodes in their lives; St. Sergius of Radonezh, St. Kiril of Beloozersk, and familiar "miracle workers" furnished subjects not derived from Byzantine art. In depicting the life of a saint, the artist found it necessary to reproduce also all that surrounded him, so that types, clothing, churches, landscape, all had to be Russian. Some of these icons, dating from the time of the death of the saint, were no doubt efforts to show him as he actually looked.

The period was marked by the development of literary taste influenced by the large diffusion of ecclesiastical literature, as well as by moral, biographical, and historical works. Side by side with tracts dealing with problems of church doctrine appeared mystical interpretations of various passages of Holy Writ and the Apocrypha. Painting, therefore, was faced with the task of expressing this new interest in its own terms, and the illustrative element clearly begins to appear in the art of this century. The icon ceases to be merely the symbolic representation of the other world. New iconographic subjects appear; some illustrate the mystical interpretation of the church dogmas; others represent parables and legends, and are therefore imbued with a didactic, moral aim. Characteristics of the Byzantine and Novgorodian traditions are interwoven with the Moscow trend, as well as with certain elements of the Renaissance from the West.

After the great fire of 1547, which nearly destroyed Moscow, it was necessary to paint new icons for the Cathedral of the Annunciation. Artists were brought from Pskov and Novgorod to do the work, and some of the new icons were painted in a manner contrary to the traditions of the old masters. This and a number of other related social and religious tendencies had a disturbing effect. The tsar found it necessary to convene a council of the wisest clergy, bring before it a list of all the various abuses visible in church and state, and devise means of reforming them. The council— which became known as the Council of One Hundred Chapters (*Stoglav Sobor*)—undertook a number of measures to establish orthodoxy in art and ritual. It published a series of general regulations dealing with icon painting: icon painters "should be humble and mild men, not given to vain words, living piously, not indulging in quarrels or drink, keeping their souls pure, and living under the supervision of their spiritual guides." The painters were formed into something like a guild subordinate to the ecclesiastical authorities; the bishops of every district were directed to "insist relentlessly that the master painters, all craftsmen and their pupils, should copy ancient patterns and not paint the Deity out of their own inventions." In the direction of idealization of types, the most they were allowed was to copy Rublev's style, which thus was perpetuated throughout the sixteenth century. In exercising the power of a political centralizing state, then, Moscow subordinated to its authority and its tradition both the artists and the art of the Novgorod and Pskov schools.

The fire of 1547 caused enormous damage to the Kremlin palace; roofs were burned out and the gilded *terem* chambers were gutted. By order of the Tsar the palace was rebuilt, and its exterior was decorated with carvings and statuary. Barberini, who visited Moscow in 1565, states that the roof of Ivan's palace was gilt. Another traveler, Mikhalon Litvin, writes that the palace was adorned with Greek statues in the manner of Phidias. The walls and vaulting of this palace, known as the Middle Golden, were frescoed in 1553 under the direction of the priest Sylvester, who was influential in the religious and moral upbringing of the boy Ivan.

The Russian historian Miliukov points out that at this time the state, to its own glorification, was collecting Russian Orthodox relics from every part of the country. The Metropolitan Makari ordered all icon painters to be brought from Novgorod and Pskov to Moscow. These painters, working in the shops of the Oruzheinaia Palata (Armory Office) under the general supervision of the tsar and his close advisers, developed their own school of painting. They introduced a series of allegorical and historical themes, glorifying the power and wisdom of the tsar, teaching obedience and humility, and bringing into Russian art an element of worldliness that clashed with the sacred quality. This opened new horizons for individual creation, freed art from the chains of ecclesiastical tradition, and made it more national and essentially much more Russian in feeling.

The frescoes and ornamentation of the Golden Chamber (Zolotaya Palata) are of special interest. These decorations show a change not only in direction, turning the Byzantine iconographic tradition towards feeling and expression, but in the very types—from Greek to Russian; most strikingly, these decorations exemplify the characteristic trait of the epoch— the subservience of painting to the general directives of the central government. Here for the first time secular subjects appear in paintings having a definite program character and literary content.

The celebrated icon painter Simon Ushakov and another court official left a detailed description of the frescoes as they existed at the end of the seventeenth century. Sacred and profane subjects were intermingled in the wall paintings of the chamber. They depicted scenes from the Bible as well as the earth with its waters and winds; the fiery circle of the sun and the circle of the moon; the air in the shape of a maiden; time winged with the four seasons; the circle of the creation; the sainted Russian princes; the baptism of St. Vladimir and Russia; scenes from the life of Vladimir Monomakh; the story of Princes Boris and Gleb; and the edifying figures of Chastity, Reason, Purity, and Righteousness.

The corridor frescoes contain an entire theory of government. The tsar, youthful in appearance, is extolled as a righteous judge and fearless warrior; he distributes alms to the poor; from his hands flows water that sanctifies the people; he vanquishes impious foes. The inspirer of this series of pictures for molding the mind and heart of the tsar (thought to have been the priest Sylvester) is depicted in the guise of a wise hermit who acts as the young ruler's mentor.

These allegorical frescoes were quite a distinct innovation, and many persons were offended, particularly by the nude and seminude figures. One "wench with naked arms, dancing with abandon," intended to represent "Lust," caused a storm. Viskovaty (Ivan IV's state secretary) indignantly expressed to the Tsar his doubts concerning the merits of the new trend in icon painting in general and of the frescoes in particular. He resented the artists' painting "according to their own understanding and not according to sacred writings." However, Viskovaty dwelled only on minor details, his criticism evidently being aimed at annoying his rival,

Sylvester. In 1554 an ecclesiastical council was convened to settle the matter, and the Metropolitan Makari succeeded in having Viskovaty's objections withdrawn.

The frescoes of Ivan's Golden Chamber reveal the influence of German and Italian-Flemish engravings. From this time on the influence of Western engraving on Russian painting grew steadily. These frescoes were in effect the precursors of those that appeared a century later on the walls of the Yaroslavl churches.

Ivan's successor, his son Feodor, exhibited no less taste for the arts and zeal for their development. The number of painters, workers in mosaics and gold, embroiderers, lapidaries, and enamelers increased rapidly. The historian Karamzin writes that the Greek Archbishop Arsenius, who accompanied the Constantinople Patriarch Jeremiah on his visit to the court of the tsar in 1588, was amazed to see the exquisite mosaics on the walls of the Irene Palace (also known as the Small Golden Tsaritsa Palace) and the many enormous gold and silver vases, some in the shape of animals such as unicorns, lions, bears, stags, pelicans, swans, pheasants, and peacocks. These vases, so heavy that twelve men could carry them only with difficulty, were manufactured in Moscow.

During the reign of Feodor Ivanovich and the regency of Boris Godunov, the chamber of the Granovitaya Palata (Palace of Facets) was decorated with frescoes similar to those in the Golden Palace. According to Ushakov, who restored the paintings in 1663, these frescoes also contained a mélange of biblical and quasi-historical subjects, edifying parables, and allegorical figures. Legendary scenes linking the Muscovite rulers with a representative of the world's oldest monarchy—Augustus Caesar—were allotted even more space, and political significance was highly stressed. One scene shows the aging Augustus Caesar "organizing the world" and sending his own brother Prus to the banks of the Vistula—the country that was thereafter called "Prus." Rurik, supposedly a fourteenth-generation descendant of the Roman Prus was invited to be prince of Rus'. Hence Ivan the Terrible's claim that his family was descended from Augustus Caesar. Another scene depicts the Byzantine Emperor Constantine Monomakh sending the imperial regalia to the Kievan Prince Vladimir. Tsar Feodor Ivanovich, wearing his crown and dressed in imperial robes, is seated on his throne; at the right stands Boris Godunov magnificently attired. They are flanked by many boyars in their colorful *kaftans* and caps. The innovation is characteristic of the Moscow School, which from that time became more and more independent of the Novgorod School, setting itself to the study of nature and the human form. While Novgorod, imbued with the old traditions, was adhering to dark flesh tints, idealization of expression, simplicity of composition, and close harmony between its figures and background, Moscow strove for picturesqueness, used warmer colors, more accurately portrayed human forms, and endowed human features with a certain grace and worldly expression.

The Ushakov frescoes remained on the walls of the Granovitaya Palata for over two centuries. But the years and the elements took their toll, and in 1881 the faded and damaged frescoes were repainted by the brothers V. and I. Belousov of the Palekh Sofonov Studio.

Survivals of the grand style could still be found, but more and more rarely as time passed. About the end of the sixteenth century, however, came another renaissance, and the dying flame flared up bright and clear; a school of artists

arose which, though its work was highly decorative and full
of elaborate ornament, nevertheless produced paintings of
inimitable beauty. This was the so-called Stroganov School,
bearing the name of a wealthy Novgorodian family which
acquired unique economic and political significance in Russia
at this time. The Stroganovs were liberal patrons of religious
art. These merchant princes, aptly called Russian Medicis,
encouraged a particular manner of icon painting in dimin-
utive size and with an elaborate execution of details, in the
spirit of Persian miniatures. Undoubtedly, examples of oriental art in various media had captured the eye of these broad-
minded lovers of art.

The principal innovations introduced by the Stroganov
School were a lavish use of gold in the rendering of vestments
and accessories. Outstanding features of the school are the
elegant attitudes of the figures and the Eastern flavor of the
colors. The pigments in common use are vermilion, brown-
red, buff-green, brownish yellow, pale pink, orange pink,
and gold. Certain peculiarities of racial type, type of buildings, hills, and vegetation are common to the whole school.
Even more frequently, purely Russian highly fanciful architectural motifs are introduced. Whenever animals appear in
the composition, their treatment is oriental. Like the Moscow
painters, the Stroganov masters drew heavily upon the legacy
bequeathed by Dionysius. Their art has much in common
with that of his sixteenth-century followers and is thus related to the Moscow School of icon painting. The icons are
small, of great technical skill, and as a rule, depict personal
rather than formal religious feelings.

The main tendency of this school, which arose in a period
when artisans' methods were increasingly invading the domain of icon painting, was to retain art on the level and in

144

the channel of the old traditions. This was also rendered necessary by the growing influx of Western innovations.

The combination of the Stroganov technique and the Moscow thematic material produced a characteristic and easily recognizable style of icon. For a better understanding of the confluence of these two currents, it is necessary to keep in mind the extensive range of subjects treated by the Moscow painters. A definite cycle of subjects was centered on the Apocalypse. Storytelling was a favorite motif of the Moscow artist, and the striking visions of the Revelations lent themselves excellently to a pictorial narrative.

At the beginning of the seventeenth century Russia was passing through a crucial period of troubles (*Smutnoe Vremya*). The years of strife and devastation ended with the election of Mikhail Romanov in 1613 to start a new dynasty. With the consolidation of Russia under a new ruler, the political role of the Stroganovs came to an end. While members of this family continued to be interested in ecclesiastical art, many of the Stroganov artists joined the ranks of the special studios created in Moscow by the Tsar for maintaining the painting of icons on the highest possible level.

During the reign of Tsar Mikhail there appeared at the court of Moscow some foreign masters, Poles and Germans, who were commissioned to paint both pictures and portraits. After the 1640's there was a continuous influx of foreign masters, whose many Russian pupils introduced Western standards into icon painting.

The inroads of Western ways of painting into the world of the icon were made by the followers of the so-called "Friaz" (Slavic corruption of "Frank") style. The timid experimentation with the art of the Friaz was probably a bold adventure for young artists who had never dared, therefore, to approach such innovations. Friaz art was the abomination of the conservative Orthodox, who saw in the new manner a heretical desecration of holy standards.

In the second half of the seventeenth century, when the extensive works of restoring the frescoes in the Cathedral of the Assumption and those of the Archangel Michael were undertaken (1653, 1657, 1660), the tsar issued a strict decree ordering the artists who still remained in the northwest to be sent to Moscow. Skilled icon painters received steady work and yearly salaries and became the accredited icon and picture painters of the tsar. They were subordinated to the Oruzheinaia Palata, which had control of everything relative to the tsar's household. A number of young people were apprenticed to these artists, and thus towards the second half of the seventeenth century the Tsar's Icon-Painting School was born.

A state art policy was inaugurated, and a special department of arts was set up, forming an annex to the Kremlin Oruzheinaia Palata. Serious discussions were held on such subjects as what should art be, what are its ideals, and what are the means of achieving them? The painters employed in this department worked out a new aesthetic and constituted a new school styled the "Tsar's School." They searched for a fresh way of expressing the old traditional ideals of religious painting. They were intrigued with the realistic representation of things and interested in rendering the palpable, in both volume and color.

A typical representative of the Tsar's School was Simon Ushakov (1626–86), deemed by some nineteenth-century Russian art historians a Slavic Raphael. He was appointed court painter at the early age of twenty-one and, like Cellini in Italy, became the darling of the mighty and the rich.

Brought up in the school of ancient tradition, he had adopted
the new outlook, and by fusing it with the tradition, had
succeeded in creating his own style. Fascinated by Western
religious art, he attempted to produce naturalistic illustrations of the Bible. The best known of the latter, his woodcut
depicting *Man's Seven Deadly Sins* is remarkable for its
vigor and conviction, but his icons are somewhat marred by
excessive sentimentality. The faces of his saints are rendered
in chiaroscuro and the figures are draped in Byzantine folds,
while the architectural settings were transformed by his collaborators, Kazanets and Kondratiev, into fanciful baroque
intricacies.

Another outstanding artist of the period was Emelian
Moskvitin, especially known for the richness and harmony
of his palette, original tastes, and freedom of technique. The
term "Emelian manner" was applied not only to his works
but also to icons executed in a similar spirit. In his art is a
belated echo of the Dionysius murals of Therapont.

The art of the Stroganov and the Tsar's Painters schools
found its highest expression in the works of Procopius
Chirin, a member of a family of many artists. He was active
in Moscow from 1620 to about 1642 and achieved great fame
for his purity of tones, smooth shading in the treatment of
facial features, and a sumptuous richness in the depiction of
patterned garments. His work exemplifies some of the
characteristic traits of the transition period between the old
styles of Novgorod and Moscow and the new painting of
the Tsar's School.

The simplicity and moderation which had endured
through centuries began to be lost. The broad planes and the
monumental feeling of the image, the classical rhythm and
the antique purity and strength of color disappear in a pas-

sion for complexity and abundance of details. Excessive attention to the rich brocades in which the images are clothed reflects the growth of a more worldly and materialistic spirit, while the ornate detail and rich color schemes suggest their affinity to oriental, especially Persian, painting. This period is a turning point in Russian iconography. The treatment rather than the religious meaning of the icon assumes the dominant role.

These icons are distinguished by a profusion of detail in their elaborate settings and exceedingly decorative backgrounds. The abundance of architectural features representing the churches and new buildings of Moscow is especially evident. On the other hand, landscapes are handled decoratively instead of naturalistically. Cities are represented as bundles of bulbous domes and sharp church spires, pale blue stripes stand for clouds, brown streaks represent the earth, and fire is depicted as a red mass with tongues of flame. The saints have the ruddy, strong-boned faces of the Muscovites, and the colors range from blood-reds to browns with black shadows. Paul Muratov points out that "in such icons the main thing is no longer in what is represented, but in the enrichments and patterns, the elaborate shale of the ground and the excessively detailed drawing of star-like flowers upon their stalks, in curls, and tiny clouds filling the grey-blue vault of heaven."

This process of secularization continued throughout the seventeenth century, gaining particular impetus from the great schism (*raskol*) which occurred in the middle of that century, discussed earlier in Chapter I. The Patriarch Nikon favored a mild form of modernism in the painting of icons, while Tsar Aleksei, father of the great innovator Peter I, strove helplessly to keep a middle course between his own personal sympathies for a more lifelike treatment of the saints and a loyal devotion to strict Orthodoxy. The very first deviations from the traditional in icon painting and minor religious observances prompted conservatives to reject all innovations of this kind.

Both Tsar and Patriarch wanted reform, each for reasons of his own, but the first advocated going about it quietly, without unnecessarily enraging the Old Believers. The Patriarch, on the other hand, wanted to crush the schism and eradicate everything connected with it, including the old religious texts and the old icons. To justify his iconoclasm Nikon afterwards told the people of Moscow that the style of the destroyed icons was "imported by Germans from the German land." It is clear that Nikon was attacking what to him was a new and dangerous departure in icon painting. His objections and those of his opponent, the leader of the Old Believers, Archpriest Avvakum, were directed against the wave of naturalism. But Avvakum especially denounced the realistic treatment of saintly personages in icons. To him the whole matter of venerating the icons was at stake, and he accused Nikon of heresy. In one of his epistles he wrote: "God hath allowed the wrong makers of icons to multiply in our land. They paint the image of Immanuel the Saviour with plump face, red lips, dimpled fingers, and large, fat legs and thighs, and altogether make him look like a German, fat-bellied and corpulent, only omitting to paint a sword at His side . . . And all this was invented by the dirty cur, Nikon, who contrived to represent holy figures on the icons in the Friaz or German manner."

Avvakum even went so far as to invent various extravagancies, such as: Our Lord with a beard at His Nativity, Our Lady pregnant at the Annunciation, Our Lord with full draperies upon the cross, as being found among the pagan Franks. He used these means to rouse his followers and dissuade them from having anything to do with the heretical icons. Thus it was mainly within the communities of the Old Believers that the ancient icon paintings were not only reverently guarded, but continued.

Tsar Aleksei stood between the old and new worlds. Desiring to pursue a progressive course in artistic matters, he invited many foreign artists and craftsmen to Russia. These artists, quite naturally, brought along with them their own art concepts, methods, and techniques, and thus were instrumental in spreading contemporary Western ideas among their Russian colleagues. Toward the end of the seventeenth century a whole new generation of Russian artists was being educated on new principles.

With the gradual disappearance of Byzantine traditions, popular art remained the only living source of inspiration for church decoration. But by the end of the seventeenth century this art also came to an end, and with the reign of Peter the Great Russian art entered upon a new historical period and began to take its place in European development.

CHAPTER SIX

THE MOSCOW SCHOOL OF DECORATIVE ARTS

Decorative Arts and Artisans

T‍HE decorative arts and crafts of Muscovite Russia constitute one of the most varied and extensive categories of the art of that period. The demand for objects of symbolic and utilitarian value was at its height during the sixteenth and seventeenth centuries; and it was the employment of such objects by the church that brought about the creation of some of the finest examples in the arts of gold and silver work, enameling, book illumination, embroidery, and carving. It is known that many such objects of great intrinsic value, highly venerated for their religious association, have been destroyed or melted down for the sake of the precious metals used in making them; but the number still in existence is very great, enabling us to infer a very large production of first-rate works, especially during the reigns of Ivan IV, Boris Godunov, and Aleksei Mikhailovich Romanov.

The role that the church played in fostering the decorative arts was highly important. Icons and iconostases were frequently decorated with frames and encasements of precious metals. The wood frames of the iconostases and their Royal Doors were richly carved or, when made of bronze, were gold-plated. Altars were covered or enclosed with lavishly ornamented panels of gold and silver. Relics of saints were enshrined in sumptuous caskets of enameled gold or carved ivory. Gospels and prayer books used for the liturgical services in the cathedrals or the private chapels of the tsar and the great nobles were bound in elaborately tooled leather covers decorated with ivory plaques, filigree work of gold, silver, and precious stones. The vestments of the patriarchs, metropolitans, and officiating priests were richly embroidered, and among the altar cloths, icon covers, and the shrouds of Christ are many superb pieces of the art of needlework. Every great cathedral possessed magnificent thrones of carved wood or gilded bronze in which the patriarch and the tsar sat during the service. The Divine Liturgy was celebrated in the sumptuous setting of the gilded iconostases, the shimmering silver lamps and flickering candles, the gold and jewels of the altar, and the gorgeous vestments of the clergy.

Among the crafts, the goldsmith's work occupied first place. The magic of gold and precious stones inspired the Russian craftsman to use these costly materials in the service of the church. Ecclesiastical jewelry is frankly designed for richness of effect; extensive surfaces of precious metals are displayed, gems are large and dazzling in color, designs are well executed, and the color effects produced by the precious stones and enamels are harmonious. The decoration is based on the principles of flat design in sharply contrasted colors and is infused with the spirit of the Orient. The human figure is freely used in the representation of religious subjects. Ornament consists largely of foliate designs and scrolls; a relation with similar designs in textiles or decorative sculpture is apparent. Gems and pearls enrich the more precious objects; the gems in box settings or gold cells, the pearls threaded on gold wire to form borders around medallions or compartments or as frame edgings.

One of the unique and interesting specialties of the art of the Moscow goldsmiths was the decorative encasement (*oklad*) of icons. This custom of enriching the painted image with gold and jewels became a thoroughly established tradition. Spurred by the pious zeal of the donors and yielding to the general taste for opulent backgrounds, the goldsmiths began adorning the icons with precious metal plaques that were embossed, chiseled, or engraved with arabesques, or nielloed or enameled in color on a silver or gold background and studded with precious stones and pearls. The borders of the frames were covered with similar silver strips that were often set with jewels. The flat golden nimbus of early times was given relief as a halo and adorned with *repoussé* or with filigree or twisted gold wire sometimes picked out with enamel; later the halo became an actual crown. But the zeal of the donors did not stop at these symbolic ornaments. The artists began to decorate icons with silver-gilt collars in the symbolic form of crescents, with pendants attached to them. To the halos they began to add earrings and strings of precious gems to hang along the forehead. The passion for magnificence and opulence in the design of religious objects became truly extravagant.

As early as the fourteenth century, under Greek influence, the Russians began to cover even the figures in the icons with plates of silver, showing in more or less relief the outlines and folds of the clothes and vestments. Such a plate (*riza*— properly speaking, a religious vestment) was first applied to the large stationary icons and later to those that individuals received as gifts at baptism or on special occasions. Paul of Aleppo described the icons in the Uspensky Cathedral: "All around the church and about the four piers are set great icons of which you can see nothing but the hands and faces. Hardly any of the clothing can be distinguished [i.e., the painting]; the rest is thick *repoussé* silver and niello. . . . Even more opulent were the trappings of the icons in the Cathedral of the Annunciation [the favorite church of the wives and daughters of the tsars]. No goldsmith, however skilled, could evaluate the great stones, diamonds, rubies and emeralds, set upon the icons and haloes of Our Saviour and Our Lady; the jewels glow in the darkness like burning coals. The gilding of the icons with pure gold, the many-hued enamel executed with the finest art, all arouses the admiration of the discerning observer. The value of the icons in this church would fill several treasuries."

The outstanding examples of ecclesiastical metal craftsmanship are the various articles and vessels used in the preparation and celebration of the Holy Eucharist, as prescribed by the Orthodox church: the chalice, the paten, the astericos used to cover the paten, a star-shaped object with rays bent to form feet, and the spoon used with the chalice, the basins, and ewers—all of chiseled or enameled gold. A number of other objects were used during the liturgical services or great ceremonial processions; censers, ciboria, reliquaries, crucifixes, croziers, banners, and processional lanterns. These were all given special attention in careful workmanship and lavish decoration.

The prayer books, the Gospels, and the Psalters were of exceptional magnificence. Their design was an art and a handicraft which involved the services of calligraphers, printers, illuminators, miniaturists, jewelers, leatherworkers, and bookbinders who worked in the Oruzheinaya Palata. In the ornamentation of sacred books a great deal of freedom and originality was shown. Russian illuminators borrowed from many sources, but in adapting diverse foreign elements, they transformed them and stamped them with their own national genius.

The earliest Slavonic ornamental motifs are characterized by arabesques of pointed ivy-shaped leaves with curled-in edges, in greens, blues, and reds on a gold ground, heightened with white for the reds and blues, yellow for the greens, and combined with thin stalks in blue, forming a flowery geometrical combination. The ornaments consist of initial letters, head- and tail-pieces and borders often bearing on the upper part figures of birds or grotesques.

To the end of the fourteenth century belong two remarkable manuscripts—the "Evangel [Gospels] of the Boyar Koshka" and the "Evangel of the Boyar Khitrovo." Both are beautifully executed and ornamented on parchment. Lazarev ventures the opinion that both of them came from the Moscow studio of Theophanes the Greek.

The Koshka Evangel has no miniatures. It is decorated with chapter heads and initials in which foliage is skillfully combined with fantastic animal bodies. Dragons, birds, dolphins, and snakes are vividly and realistically rendered. The initials have a jewel-like finish; their pure bright colors— golden, blue, green, and red are remarkable for their brilliancy. The volume has gorgeous silver covers richly decorated with *repoussé* work, filigree, and enamels. It is one of the great fourteenth-century masterpieces of the art of book designing and book binding.

No less great is the "Khitrovo Evangel"—the gift of Tsar Feodor Alekseevich to the boyar Khitrovo (superintendent of the Kremlin Armory shops in 1654–80). We do not know who were its creators, but its design, craftsmanship, and style of decoration all point to Theophanes the Greek. There are, however, a number of Russian art historians—among them Alpatov—who think that some of the miniatures were painted by Rublev.

The Khitrovo Evangel differs from the Koshka; it is decorated not only with chapter heads and initials but also with miniatures representing the four Evangelists and their symbols (the Eagle, the Angel, the Bull, and the Lion). The capital letters are drawn in the form of birds, dolphins, and snakes. Especially finely rendered is the drawing of a blue heron standing on a snake and staring at it.

The finest miniature in the Khitrovo Evangel is the figure of a curly-haired angel with a book in his hand, symbolizing the Apostle Matthew. It is a figure of youthful charm and grace in motion. Book in hand, he is shown moving swiftly over the edge of the frame, his broad wing lightly spread out behind him, so that he seems to be soaring. The figure is fitted into the round frame with a subtle sense of proportion; and the flowing lines of the folds in the robe complement the round frame. This miniature seems to have all the earmarks of Rublev's genius. Another miniature in this manuscript is that of an eagle symbolizing the Apostle John. The bird, however, looks more like a gentle dove than an eagle, the only acquiline feature being its curved beak. Its wings are slightly lifted, in its claws it holds a book, and, poised within the round frame, it appears in flight. Thus, the legendary symbol of John came to appear in this manuscript as a prophetic bird.

The close of the fifteenth century and the century following are the richest periods of Russian illuminated manuscripts. They show a creative vitality and a fertile inventiveness in a great variety of ornamental motifs. Persian, Arabic, Indian—all the splendor of the Eastern styles mingled with much that was borrowed from Western sources. All that was combined, transformed, and resolved into something quite original and unique, something that had a flavor all of its own.

The elaborately embroidered vestments of the clergy, the altar cloths and icon covers, the palls and shrouds of Christ used on specific occasions are a further illustration of the practice established by the church in educating the masses by means of pictorial representation. The composition subjects, largely from Byzantine tradition, include religious scenes like the Annunciation and the Lamentation. Although the message is conveyed in the language of the art of Byzantium, the accent is decidedly Russian. The solemnity and beauty of the Byzantine models must have captured the imagination of the Russian artist, and he was quick to recognize their artistic merit and accept their underlying principles and techniques. But here again, as in the other branches of art, he set out to assimilate and transform the Byzantine models and imbue them with his own spirit.

To students of Muscovite culture, old Russian embroidery has an additional and very special interest because it is the creation of feminine hands of old Russia, a profoundly revealing expression of the spiritual and emotional nature of the Russian woman secluded in her convent or *terem*; it demonstrates the zeal, taste, and skill not only of the convent-trained nun, but also of the staff embroiderers in the workshops of the grand princely courts.

The many technical problems encountered in embroidery make it one of the most difficult of arts. It was the icon painter who usually outlined the general composition of the picture, but it was the woman needleworker who did the embroidery. From the moment she took over the design, she must have had a full appreciation of the problems involved— technical as well as artistic; and at the very first threading of her needle it was necessary for her to visualize fully the finished product as it might be affected by the combined result of texture, thread, stitch, hue, and sheen of her media. Many of the extant needlework pictures often rival in conception, beauty, and technique the paintings which adorned the iconostases and walls of the churches.

An outstanding example of historical and artistic interest is the icon cover used to decorate the Rublev icon of *The Trinity* mentioned above. This cloth, now kept in the Zagorsk Historical Museum, was designed and embroidered in 1499 "by order of the Tsargrad [Constantinople] Tsaritsa, Grand Princess of Moscow, Sophia" (Zoë Palaeologue). A large cross with Slavonic inscriptions fills the central area of the cloth. The panels bordering the central area depict several scenes from the Gospels (Annunciation, Ascension, Descent of the Holy Spirit, and the Trinity) and scenes from the lives of various saints. This work has one peculiar feature not found in other monuments of Russian embroidery—the surfaces of the vestments, of the architectural elements, and of the trees are covered with varicolored specks. The Russian art historian A. N. Svirin ventures the opinion that this feature was borrowed from samples of Western textiles. In all probability, the Palaeologue Princess was anxious to incorporate in the decoration of this icon cover certain well-remembered Italian motifs.

More complex in composition than the icon covers are the shrouds of Christ (*plashchanitsy*). They are oblong panels of fairly large dimensions (seven to eight feet long), having a border of geometrical design or conventionalized Slavonic lettering. The shrouds are used in Orthodox churches on Good Friday as coverings for the ceremonial bier of Christ; the principal subject is the dead Christ mourned by the Virgin, the angels, and the saints. One of the finest shrouds in existence is the so-called Puchenezhskaya *Plashchanitsa* (1441). The artist resorted to extreme elongation in the portrayal of Christ's body on the shroud, although the figures of the Virgin, St. John, and the angels are of normal proportions. The device of distortion was evidently used as a means of heightening expression. The embroidery is on a background of silk; the needlework is exceptionally fine, of great simplicity, and showing exquisite taste in the choice of color. Experts consider it a superlative example of embroidery.

The church was the principal but not the sole patron of the decorative arts and crafts. Moscow's goldsmiths and other craftsmen were set a number of new tasks of a secular nature by the rising, wealthy upper layer of the city's population. Most important, life at the tsar's court and in the households of the great nobles was becoming more and more ostentatious, demanding magnificence, luxury, and color in surroundings, appointments, and personal apparel. The walls and ceilings of the palaces were covered with brilliant frescoes, and the furniture and furnishings were richly ornamented in the spirit of the time, in keeping with the decorative vogues of church furnishings and the architecture of "Imperial" Moscow.

The requirements of the church and the court would have supported a large number of artists and craftsmen. But when, in addition, the many minor princely courts and the wealthy merchant houses had to be kept supplied with luxury articles of every description, sixteenth-century Moscow was compelled to summon the best artisans from every corner of the realm and invite many from various foreign countries. The city thus became the leading center of fine craftsmanship and the greatest producer of luxury goods. She held her lead in this field throughout the entire seventeenth century.

The tsar and the patriarch maintained their own workshops in the Oruzheinaya Palata staffed with artists and craftsmen skilled in the production of luxury articles. A large number of craftsmen working privately with a few helpers supplied the ever growing demands of the nobles and rich merchants for jewelry and other luxury wares.

The Oruzheinaya Palata

In the preceding pages we referred to the Oruzheinaya Palata and its contribution to the arts and crafts of Muscovite Russia. Its role in the design and manufacture of arms and armor was great, but no less great was its role as a training center of generations of icon painters, manuscript calligraphers, illuminators, miniaturists, jewelers, and many other craftsmen in the field of the decorative arts.

It does not come within the scope of this book to present a detailed history of this unique institution. However, a few of the more important events in its long life, its manifold activities, and its significant personalities, so far as they have influenced Russian decorative arts and crafts, must be singled out.

This institution, which is the oldest and richest museum of decorative art in Russia, was created in the first years of the sixteenth century as an arsenal. It became successively a technical, scientific, pedagogical, and art institute, and contained shops and studios of icon and portrait painting, gold and silversmith work, keeping at the same time its original purpose—the manufacture of arms. By 1628 some of its artifacts were already worthy of being museum pieces.

The office in charge of the tsar's treasure, organized during the reign of Ivan III and mentioned for the first time in 1494, consisted of three sections: the Grand Treasury, which contained the tsar's regalia presented to Vladimir Monomakh by the Byzantine emperor; the Armory (Oruzheinaya Palata), which housed shops for the manufacture of the tsar's arms; and the storehouse or depot that contained the imperial robes, uniforms, arms, and armor for the tsar, his bodyguards, and his most trusted military units.

Even among the first employees of the shops there were not only craftsmen skilled in arms manufacture, but also artists who specialized in the embellishment of the tsar's weapons, armor, trappings, and the imperial household vessels and plate.

In the icon painting chamber (Ikonnaya Palata), which was somewhat like the Italian l'Opera del Duomo, were artists who designed the tsar's emblems and standards and other decorative items for the tsar's immediate family. These artists also painted the frescoes in the tsar's apartments.

The manufacture of arms was at an especially high level during the reign of Aleksei Mikhailovich. The Russian craftsmen either followed the models of foreign masters or used the old Russian models as their inspiration, perfecting and elaborating them or inventing new models and decorating them in the "Moscow Style," in keeping with the rich national costumes of the period.

In Muscovite Russia the Oruzheinaya Palata, with its closely integrated gold and silversmith workshops and the private shops of the tsar and tsaritsa, was the very fountain-head of Russian national art. It was a kind of central station, where nearly everything pertaining to the arts and crafts largely originated, and from which its various products spread all over the land. Although the Oruzheinaya Palata was not exactly a stronghold of tradition—more of the latest innovations, local and foreign, could be found there than anywhere else—still its products must be considered as the "work of Moscow" (*Moskovskoe delo*)—art largely influenced by the spirit of medieval Russia.

The particular style—often of monumental character and imposing magnificence—developed by the Oruzheinaya Palata was the result of its craftsmen's study of the arts of the times of Ivan the Terrible and his predecessors. Ivan was especially influential in developing the artistic activities of the Oruzheinaya Palata. He bought stocks of precious metals and gold and silver vessels in Germany and commandeered artists and artisans skilled in embellishing icon encasements from Novgorod. He also imported craftsmen specializing in religious vessels from Riga. These craftsmen became members of the staff of the Oruzheinaya Palata, contributing their knowledge and skill to the development of the arts and crafts as well as to the further growth of weapon manufacturing. The bureau grew in importance and became firmly established as an industrial, scientific, and artistic center.

During the Time of Trouble the administration of the Oruzheinaya Palata ceased to function, and most of its artists and craftsmen deserted to the provinces. With the accession of Tsar Mikhail Feodorvich they returned to Moscow and resumed their work. Moscow came to life again, ushering in a strong revival of cultural and artistic activities.

Tsar Mikhail re-established the Oruzheinaya Palata, but concentrated mainly on the purely technical side of arms manufacturing because he felt that decoration and embellishment could wait. He imported mining engineers and technicians and built powder and firearms plants; he invited the best native and foreign specialists to his service. The bureau in charge of arms manufacturing became the most important section of the Armory. The goldsmithing and silversmithing sections were detached from arms manufacturing and functioned as separate bureaus subordinated to the arms office, in which all the industrial and artistic activities were centered—mining, smelting, casting; painting of icons, portraits, designing of emblems, blazonry, military standards, government documents, charters, and citations; miniature painting, manuscript illuminating, and bookbinding. The administration of each one of these activities, headed by a special functionary, was housed in a separate building or buildings. The buildings were close to the palace and functioned as branches of the court household.

An important period in the artistic activities of the Oruzheinaya Palata began with the appointment of boyar Bogdan Matveevich Khitrovo (1616–80) to the office of armorer. His appointment, by Tsar Aleksei Mikhailovich in 1654, to this high post coincided with the initiation of the Nikonian reforms, which had far-reaching effects on Russian history and art. The figure of Khitrovo, as an administrator and enlightened progressive is so important that it is necessary to consider both the man and the historical setting in which he moved.

Both Nikon and the Tsar wanted to introduce into the art of icon painting a current of new ideas and to bring it in line with the reforms. They also decided to reintroduce the outer and inner features of the Greek church: the basic plan, cupolas, furnishings, vessels, ambos, bishops' crosses, vestments, and cowls. For that purpose it was necessary that the head of the Icon and Goldsmith chambers should be a man who could see eye to eye with the Tsar and the Patriarch and act in agreement with them in all matters related to the Nikonian reforms.

Khitrovo happened to be the ideal man for the position. He had already distinguished himself as soldier, diplomat, judge, administrator, and builder. He was not creative, but he had a gift of sensing the problems of his artists and craftsmen. Above all, he had a knack of combining the management and co-ordination of things purely technical with those that belong to the spiritual and creative world. Although he had the greatest respect for the past, he encouraged any new expression that fitted the temper of an age when Western art was becoming firmly established in Russia.

The thorniest problem facing Khitrovo was to determine the line of demarcation between Orthodoxy and heresy in icon painting—he had to reconcile his own artistic judgment with the often divergent preferences of the Tsar and the Patriarch. On the one hand, he had to take into consideration many hallowed traditions in the treatment of religious subjects; on the other, he had to struggle with the technical difficulties peculiar to Russian religious painting, with the fact that the icon was not a creation of a single artist but the collective work of a number of specialists. Then, too, the Western influences in icon painting were antithetical to the very spirit of Russian icon painting—a folk creation, its content representing the confession of faith, its techniques the ways of the people.

Khitrovo undertook the job with energy and boldness. In

spite of the sharp protests of Nikon and the tirades of the fanatical Archpriest Avvakum, he welcomed Western influences. The works of art produced during the twenty-six years of his tenure clearly indicate that he was a man of great culture who appreciated talent and individuality in artists, giving his greatest encouragement and support to those who could value foreign models, adapt them to the needs of Russia, and imbue the finished product with the Russian spirit.

The activities of the icon chamber were not limited strictly to sacred painting; its artists also painted portraits and miniatures, illuminated manuscripts, made maps and charts, designed furniture and furnishings, created frescoes and objects of gold, designed textiles for vestments—they did everything and anything that required creative power, imagination, and ability.

The celebrated Ushakov prepared designs for a number of gold and enamel vessels in the ateliers of the Oruzheinaya Palata and also decorated arms and drew maps. His chief work at the Palata was designing church vessels to be executed in precious metals and enamels; he is thought to have been the designer of Patriarch Nikon's miter, which has some noteworthy enameling, especially in the upper part.

During the second half of the seventeenth century the ornamental patterns of a secular nature gradually underwent a change, away from the Russian and Byzantine models toward those of Western Europe. However, the floral ornamentation of manuscripts and icons was still in the ancient Russian style, featuring extensive application of gold and silver backgrounds. "Frankish" or Western ornament—the motifs and style of the baroque—was used rarely and timidly. The craft of embossing and chasing reached a high level of excellence in this period, and the objects from the tsars' and patriarchs' treasures, both religious and secular, are all outstanding examples.

The principal business of the Oruzheinaya Palata, the purely technical and industrial phase of arms manufacturing, reached a high level of competence. Along with the technical improvements in ceremonial arms, their embellishment was also greatly perfected. Here we see decorative art come to the fore. Among the artists and the craftsmen we often find the personalities already familiar to us as icon painters, book designers, illuminators, and illustrators.

During Khitrovo's tenure the arts of enameling, niello, and filigree were even more cultivated than those of gold and silver *repoussé*. They achieved a style all their own and acquired unique distinguishing characteristics of refinement and elegance—novelties in design and technique, new fashions in the application of gold and silver, unique and entirely different color schemes—all of which was reflected in the other arts and crafts of that period. The activities and innovations in this field were largely due to Tsar Aleksei Mikhailovich and express the personal tastes of the Tsar. His influence is especially revealed in two fields, gold sheet stamping and enameling. Aleksei was favorably disposed toward the Orthodox East and its representative arts. As a result, a number of jeweled articles appeared in the Tsargrad (Constantinople) style—a combination of the art of the Turkish Mussulman East with that of the Greeks and Mount Athos. The style of the Western jewelers, so much in vogue during the reign of his father, receded into the background.

The Tsargrad style in jewelry was distinctive in its extensive use of thin gold plaques and sheathing decorated with stamped Greek-Byzantine designs and enriched with emeralds, rubies, diamonds, and enamels of the same shades as the gems. This style, in great favor throughout Aleksei's reign, seems to have been peculiar to his epoch.

In the art of enameling, the influence of Aleksei's tastes reveals itself in his partiality toward the colors green, blue, and white, with the frequent addition of yellow and sometimes of red shades. During his reign pink Turkish foliage designs and flowers also appeared in the enamel ornamentation. These same pink flowers can be seen in the illuminations and page borders of manuscripts and in the design of chapter heads, citations, charters, and patents of nobility. Aleksei's preference for green tints was so strong as to influence even the architectural decoration of his day—for example, the exterior wall murals of the Poteshnyi Palace.

Partly under the influence of Mount Athos and with the help of Greek craftsmen, niello work reached a high level of development. This art was long known in Russia, but it was rarely used except for very fine lines in ornament and inscriptions. During the reign of Tsar Aleksei it was more frequently and widely applied in gold and silver work. Niello was often used to cover the entire background and thus became the forerunner of the niello ground that was so much in vogue during the Moscow period of Peter the Great's reign.

The Oruzheinaya Palata with its many shops continued to develop and prosper until 1707. The last armorer was Prince Peter Ivanovich Prozorovsky. In 1711, Peter I ordered the personnel of the Oruzheinaya Palata transferred from Moscow to the newly established armory in St. Petersburg. All the designers and craftsmen in any way connected with the arts went along. The year 1711 is considered by many historians as the darkest year in the history of Russian national art. The Russian art historian V. K. Trutovsky writes: "The most remarkable artistic institution, the only one of its kind, in the truest sense of the word, an institution, the like of which never existed anywhere or at any time, was destroyed with a single stroke of the pen, with the scribble of five letters [Peter]. With it died the very heart of national Russian art. It never beat again and there was never a true renaissance. It carried with it to its grave the old traditions, originality, and uniqueness which so powerfully and brilliantly informed all its creations, subjugating everything foreign and external: the art of the Franks [*friazheskoe*], of Byzantium [Tsargrad or Constantinople], Persia, and Venice. It carried with it to the grave the very spirit and sensitivity of the Russian artistic soul."

FOR nearly four hundred years, until 1713 when Peter the Great transferred the seat of government to St. Petersburg, Moscow was the capital of Russia, the seat of the Orthodox faith, the custodian and guiding center of Russia's literary and artistic life, and the principal trade and commercial metropolis of the realm.

Politically and culturally Moscow had supplanted Kiev and Vladimir and had taken the leadership over Tver, Novgorod, and Pskov. She developed into a powerful community which maintained contacts with other centers of civilization, fought for its political existence, conducted a hard struggle for the unity of the Muscovite state, and gained everlasting fame in repeatedly acting as a center of national resistance to foreign invaders: first in 1380 when the Muscovite army under the command of Grand Prince Dmitri Donskoy defeated the Tatar horde at Kulikovo, and again in 1612 when the Polish army reduced the greater part of the city to ashes before being driven out. Two hundred years later the city, at a frightful cost, again became the center of successful resistance to the Napoleonic invasion.

Regardless of wars, pestilence, innumerable fires, and civil strife, Moscow was able to maintain her greatness, her lead over the rival cities, and retain the admiration and affection of the Russian people long after she ceased to be the political capital of the realm. The nineteenth-century Slavophiles, who held that Russia was the home of a native Slav tradition—higher in many respects than European civilization—cherished the grandiose dream that Moscow, as the "Third Rome," would become the source of enlightenment and regeneration not only for a decadent West-infected Russia but for all of Europe.

The city itself is a veritable museum of Russian civilization. Within its limits we can follow the development of Russian architecture in an unbroken line from the still standing small log cabins hidden in the narrow winding side streets, the sixteenth- and seventeenth-century churches and palaces in the Kremlin, the eighteenth- and nineteenth-century classical mansions, the skyscrapers, administration and commercial buildings of the Stalin era, to the modern buildings of the late 1950's. The Kremlin is not only one of the greatest monuments of Old Russian architecture, it is also one of Russia's richest treasure houses of decorative art. The treasure of the Kremlin is in many ways a chronicle of the aesthetic development of the country. It contains a history in precious metals and jewels as well as in the stones and bricks of the walls and towers.

The eighteenth century, notably its first half, was a period of decline in the architectural activities of Moscow and of advancing decay of the Kremlin. Peter the Great, who detested Moscow and what it represented, was busy building a new capital. All his energies and resources that could be spared from waging war were concentrated on the establishment of a new center of Russian civilization. Moscow and the Kremlin, associated in his mind with the bitter memories and frightful events of his boyhood, were purposely neglected. Not until after 1750 did the government do anything concrete about replanning the old capital, widening its streets, and reviving the dying Kremlin.

The building of palaces and churches in Moscow was resumed on a large scale under Peter's successors. The early part of the eighteenth century and the reigns of Anna and Elizabeth witnessed the construction of a new imperial court center at Lefortovo on the Yauza. Empress Anna (1730–40) built a wooden palace there which was rebuilt several times in later years. Big masonry mansions sprang up along the route from the Kremlin and Kitai-Gorod to the new palace. The architectural style of the palaces and churches built at that time was preeminently baroque. But the Moscow architects directed this architectural trend in a manner that linked it strongly with seventeenth-century Moscow architecture.

Toward the end of the eighteenth century, Russian architecture, having become definitely classic, branched off into two schools: the solemn monumental Petersburgian and the more intimate Muscovian. Moscow looked upon life and art in a way peculiarly its own, and expressed in its artistic creations elements totally different from those favored in the capital. Moscow the aged, in contrast to Petersburg the young, followed its own bent architecturally, and the very determination of the Muscovites to live in the way they found most comfortable, whatever the aesthetic watchword of the day might be, gave the characteristic Moscow house the charm of sheer naturalness and made Moscow the most picturesque city in the Empire.

At a time when Petersburg was engaged mainly in building palaces and monumental public and government buildings, Moscow more often was building private residences and smaller palaces. Petersburg, set amidst forest clearings and marshes, was creating and fashioning its own architectural background and landscape. Moscow, putting up its classical palaces alongside its old Kremlin, made the most of an already existing city background. Generally speaking, Moscow yielded to Petersburg in range and scale of construction but invariably outstripped the newer city in colorfulness, originality, and intimacy.

Stylistically, Moscow architecture is marked by an attempt to soften the forms of European classicism by giving them a freer and more colorful treatment. A characteristic architectural feature of the private palaces built at that time was the combination of the grand style of a metropolis with the typical features of the country houses. Even in the very large Pashkov mansion (now a branch of the Lenin Library) traces of country estate planning are clearly to be discerned. There is the same division into a main building from which long corridors run to the wings and the big yard with stables, coach houses, service buildings, and the large gardens which usually surrounded these aristocratic palaces.

Moscow's appearance again underwent a fundamental change at the beginning of the nineteenth century, when it was rebuilt after the fire of 1812. Unity was introduced in the motley assortment of middle-class private dwellings when the government-appointed commission for replanning and general design supervision restricted the choice of architectural elements to be used on façades, the columns of the portico, window and door frames, sculptured details, and gateways. Various combinations of these elements ensured both variety and a degree of unity among the private middle-class dwellings.

Attempts to bring order into the layout of the ancient city

were continued in the first half of the nineteenth century. The most important steps in this direction were: the formation of several squares and broad avenues around Kitai-Gorod, the confining of the Neglinnaya River in a subterranean tube, the laying out of Alexandrovsky Park along the Kremlin west wall, and the creation of more boulevards along the route of the Belgorod wall. At the same time the former earthen rampart which encircled Moscow was replaced by broad streets. This circular arrangement of the streets gave final shape to the radial layout of Moscow, the beginnings of which date back to the sixteenth century.

The transfer of the capital back to Moscow immediately after the 1917 revolution restored the city to the position she had always occupied in the eyes of the Russian people. After a lapse of two centuries, she again resumed her role as the cultural capital of Russia, and the Kremlin once more became the nerve center of the land.

SELECTED BIBLIOGRAPHY

Contemporary Sources in English and in Translation

Chancellor, Richard. *Description of Muscovy in the 16th Century*, in R. Hakluyt, *Principal Navigations and Voyages*. London, 1809.

Herberstein, S. von. *Commentaries on Muscovite Affairs*. Ed. and trans. by O. P. Backus III. Lawrence, University of Kansas, 1956. Herberstein was ambassador from Vienna to the court of the Grand Prince Vasili Ivanovich in 1517 and again in 1526. His travel notes are considered to be the first authentic description of Muscovite life based upon long residence and experience by a European observer, and are a major source of information for the period.

Olearius, Adam. *The Voyages and Travels of the Ambassador from the Duke of Holstein to the Great Duke of Muscovy, and the King of Persia, 1633–39*. Rendered into English by John Davies of Kidwelly. London, 1669. Olearius visited Russia several times as secretary to embassies sent by Frederick, duke of Holstein. While in Moscow, Olearius constantly wandered through the streets observing every phase of Muscovite activities and recording his impressions. His descriptive pen pictures of Moscow street life are perhaps the best we have.

Paul of Aleppo. *Travels of the Antioch Patriarch Macarius in Russia* (1654–1657). Moscow, 1896–1900. Translated from the Arabic into Russian. Archdeacon Paul, who accompanied the Patriarch, left a copious diary of all that occurred. It is particularly valuable as a record of the experiences and the impressions of a Syrian Orthodox Christian observing the Russian church and its clergy during the great schism.

The Kremlin and the City

Bakhrushin, S. V. and others, eds., *Period of Feudalism XII–XVII Centuries*. Vol. I in *Istoriya Moskvy*. Moscow, 1952. Nearly every aspect of the history of Moscow is discussed by various authors. The volume (778 pages) contains many illustrations, maps, and a large, detailed bibliography.

Bartenev, S. P. *Moskovskii Kreml' v starinu i teper'*. 2 vols. St. Petersburg, 1912–18. Vol. I: *Historical Outline of the Kremlin Fortifications, Walls and Towers;* Vol. II: *The Court of the First Grand Princes and Tsars of the House of Rurik*. The best books in Russian on the subject. Contains many illustrations and a good bibliography.

Moskva v yeiya proshlom i nastoyashchem. 12 vols. Moscow, 1910–17. An extensive illustrated work dealing with the various aspects of the growth and development of the Kremlin and Moscow from their legendary beginnings to the twentieth century. Contains essays on the geology and topography of the city's location, its political and commercial significance in the upbuilding of the Russian state, and the life and customs of its temporal and spiritual rulers and of its inhabitants through the centuries.

Tikhomirov, M. N. *Srednevekovaya Moskva v XIV–XV*

vekakh. Moscow, 1957. A scholarly, well-documented history of medieval Moscow.

Voyce, Arthur. *The Moscow Kremlin; Its History, Architecture, and Art Treasures*. Berkeley, University of California Press, 1954. A detailed study of the subject, containing many illustrations, tables, notes, and an extensive bibliography.

Zabelin, Ivan. *Istoriya goroda Moskvy*. Moscow, 1905. Written by one of the great authorities on the history of Moscow.

Art and Architecture

Bogoyavlensky, S. K. and Novitsky, G. A., eds. *Gosudarstvennaya Oruzheinaya Palata Moskovskogo Kremlya*. Moscow, 1954. A collection of articles dealing with the artistic treasures displayed in the museum of the Moscow Kremlin Armory. Contains many illustrations in color and black and white and a large detailed bibliography.

Grabar, I. E., and others, eds. *Istoriya russkogo iskusstva*. 12 vols. Moscow, 1955. A monumental, collective, richly illustrated work dealing with the development of the Russian fine and applied arts from antiquity to the present day. Volume III contains scholarly well-documented essays on the art of central Russian principalities in the thirteenth through the fifteenth centuries, the art of Grand-Princely Moscow, and the art of the centralized Russian state. Extensive, detailed bibliography.

Kondakov, N. P. *Russkaya ikona*. 4 vols. Prague, 1928–33. A comprehensive survey of Russian iconography. Contains excellent plates in color and black and white.

Krasovski, M. V. *Kurs istorii russkoi arkhitektury*. Moscow, 1911. Wooden architecture.

Muratov, P. P. *Les Icones russes*. Paris, 1927.

Réau, Louis. *L'art russe des origines à Pierre le Grand*. Paris, 1921. Vol. I of *L'Art russe*.

Solntsev, F. G., illustrator. *Drevnosti rossiiskago gosudarstva*. Moscow, 1849–53. The work contains more than five hundred colored and beautifully delineated plates illustrating the antiquities of the Russian Empire. The text is a collective work edited by Count Sergei Stroganov, Mikhail Zagoskin, Ivan Snegirev, and Alexander Veltman.

Voyce, Arthur. *Russian Architecture: Trends in Nationalism and Modernism*. New York, 1948.

Zabello, S. Ya., and others. *Russkoe derevyannoe zodchestvo*. Moscow, 1942. A comprehensive study of Russian wooden architecture. Richly illustrated.

Church and Religion

Fedotov, G. P. *The Russian Religious Mind*. Cambridge, Mass., 1946.

Golubinsky, E. *Istoriya russkoi tserkvi*. Moscow, 1881. A standard work on the history of the Russian church.

History, Literature, and Culture

Gudzii, N. K. *History of Early Russian Literature*. New York, 1949.

Kliuchevsky, V. O. *A History of Russia*. 5 vols. London–New York, 1911–31.

Miliukov, Paul. *Outlines of Russian Culture*. 3 vols. Philadelphia, 1942. Part I, *Religion and the Church*; Part II, *Literature*; Part III, *Architecture, Painting, and Music*.

Mirsky, D. S. *Russia, a Social History*. Ed. by C. G. Seligman, F.R.S. London, 1931.

Vernadsky, G. *The Mongols and Russia*. New Haven, 1953.
———. *Russia at the Dawn of the Modern Age*. New Haven, 1959.

INDEX

Index

Photius, Metropolitan: 51
Plashchanitsy: *see* Shrouds of Christ
Police Department: 76, 81
Population: 46–53
Posnik (Postnik), Yakovlev, architect: 26, 113
Poteshnyi Dvorets (Amusement Palace): 118f., 167
Potiphar's wife: 5
Prokhor, the Elder of Gorodets, icon painters: 128, 132
Prozorovsky, Peter Ivanovich: 167
Prussus (Prus), legendary brother of Augustus Caesar: 17, 143
Pskov: architects of, 105; school of painting, 128
Pulci, Luigi, Florentine poet: 14

Quarters: *see* districts or settlements

Rambaud, historian: 4
Red Square: 39, 73, 75ff., 83, 85, 111f.
Reform movement in the Russian Church: *see* Schism
Religious processions: 85f.
Reutenfels, Yakov, Rome Ambassador: 71, 83
Rhalev, Demetrios and Manuel: 18
Riza: 153
Romanov dynasty, advent of: 31
Rome: 13ff.; Second (Constantinople), 12, 15f.; Third (Moscow), 15f.
Roofs: gable, 96; tent, 101f., 108, 110, 112, 114f., 119f., 122
Rublev, Andrei: most significant figure among Russian icon painters, 129f.; early works, 130; later artistic activities, 130–31; leader in the struggle for Russia's artistic independence, 131; founder of the Moscow School of painting, 131; beatified by the Russian Orthodox church, 131–32; influence of his era, 136–37; his style copied, 139; earmarks of his genius, 156
Ruffo, Marco, Italian architect: 108
Rurik, dynasty or house of: 17, 30
Rurik, Prince of Rus: 143
Rusalki and *Rusalii*: 90

Sadovoe Ring: 44
Samoderzhets, meaning of the word: 17

Index

Sylvester, Archpriest: 26, 49

Tamerlane, Mongol chieftain: 9f.
Tatar Horde: 6, 9ff.
Tatar *sloboda*: 51
Tatar supremacy thrown off: 15
Tatars: struggle with, 4–12 *passim*
Tavern (*kabak*): 69
Tent type churches: 101ff.
Terem: 64f.
Terem Palace (*Teremnoi Dvorets*): 109; history and description of, 116–17
Teutonic Knights: 11
Theodosius (Feodosi, Feodor), icon painter: 136
Theognostus, Metropolitan: *see* Feognost
Theophanes the Greek, painter: 9, 11, 128ff.
Therapont Monastery: frescoes of the Church of the Nativity of the Virgin, 136, 147
Third Rome, theory of: 16
Three Hebrew youths in the fiery furnace, story of: 89
Tikhomirov, M. N., historian: *xi*, 10
Tile manufacturing, glazing and coloring: 57
Time of Trouble (*Smutnoe vremya*): 30, 162
Timothy, (Pope), icon painter: 136
Tokhtamysh, Tatar general: 9, 127
Tolbuzin, Simeon, Boyar: 18
Tower (Belfry) of Ivan Veliky: 106–108
Tower of Patriarch Philaret: 108
Trade associations: 47
Trade: domestic, 58–59; foreign, 59f.
Traemer, Edward: 28
Trans-Volga hermits, party of: 16
Tretyakov Gallery, Moscow: 130
Trinity, Old Testament, The (icon by Rublev): 130, 158
Trinity St. Sergius Monastery (near Moscow): 130, 134
Trinity Week, celebration of: 90
Troekurov, Prince, Moscow military governor: 75
Trutovsky, V. K., art historian, quoted: 168
Tsar, title of: 17

Index

Wooden churches: construction methods, 99f.; rectangular tradition, evolution of, 101; octagonal form, 101
Wooden cupola: 99
"Work of Moscow" (*Moskovskoe delo*): 162
Workmanship: 57

Yarets, icon painter: 136
Yaroslav the Wise: 28
Yauza River: 5, 42, 52
Yermolai-Erasmus, writer: 26
Yoachim, Patriarch: 89
Yosaf, Patriarch: 93
Yuri Dolgoruky, Grand Prince: *see* Dolgoruky
Yuri, son of Andrei Bogoliubsky: *see* Bogoliubsky
Yuriev-Polski: 4

Zabelin, Ivan, historian: *xi,* 65
Zagorodie settlement: 42
Zagorsk (near Moscow): Trinity St. Sergius Monastery at, 130
Zakomara: 100
Zaradye settlement: 47
Zarechye settlement: 42
Zemlyanoy Gorod: 44
Zemshchina: 22
Zoë, Princess Palaeologue (wife of Ivan III): *see* Sophia Fominichna
Zvenigorod: town, 130; Cathedral of the Assumption frescoes, Cathedral of the Nativity icons, 130f.

The CENTERS OF CIVILIZATION SERIES, of which this volume is the fourteenth, was inaugurated in 1959 by the University of Oklahoma Press, and is intended to include accounts of the great cities of the world during particular periods of their flowering, from ancient times to the present. The following list is complete as of the date of Publication of this volume.

1. Charles Alexander Robinson, Jr. *Athens in the Age of Pericles.*
2. Arthur J. Arberry. *Shiraz: Persian City of Saints and Poets.*
3. Glanville Downey. *Constantinople in the Age of Justinian.*
4. Roger Le Tourneau. *Fez in the Age of the Marinides.* Translated from the French by Besse Alberta Clement.
5. Henry Thompson Rowell. *Rome in the Augustan Age.*
6. Glanville Downey. *Antioch in the Age of Theodosius the Great.*
7. Richard M. Kain. *Dublin in the Age of William Butler Yeats and James Joyce.*
8. Glanville Downey. *Gaza in the Early Sixth Century.*
9. Bernard Lewis. *Istanbul and the Civilization of the Ottoman Empire.*
10. Richard E. Sullivan. *Aix-la-Chapelle in the Age of Charlemagne.*
11. Elizabeth Riefstahl. *Thebes in the Time of Amunhotep III.*
12. Nicola A. Ziadeh. *Damascus Under the Mamlūks.*
13. Edward Wagenknecht. *Chicago.*
14. Arthur Voyce. *Moscow and the Roots of Russian Culture.*